TEXAS
TRADITIONS

★

The Culture of the
Lone Star State

13 Cowgirls © Bob Wade 1979. Acrylic and oil on photo linen, 4' x 10'. Reprinted by permission and courtesy of the artist.

Little, Brown and Company

Boston   New York   Toronto   London

TEXAS TRADITIONS

The Culture of the Lone Star State

★ Robyn Montana Turner

For Tim, a Texas treasure — whose mother says
he's the sweetest boy in Texas

I'd like to extend my grateful appreciation to the many individuals who influenced the development of this book: my editor, Hilary M. Breed, for tenaciously seeing it through to completion; Linda Jamison, from whose idea the book was born; Virginia A. Creeden for gathering permissions for the images from around the state; Hannah Mahoney for copyediting; Chris Paul for design; Tara Turner for indexing; my postal carrier, Arnold Arce, for safely delivering the hundreds of images and manuscript pages to and from my office; the many Texas historians whose documents I researched; Susan M. Mayer, Michael Tracy, Stanley and Wendy Marsh III, and Bob Wade for so generously permitting us to include images of their works of art; Paramount Publishing Company, Texana Conn, and Carolyn Kuhn for graciously supplying colorful primary source materials; and Larry Willoughby for reviewing the manuscript. Many organizations and institutions devoted substantial time and labor to the making of this book: Barker Texas History Center, the Institute of Texan Cultures, Texas Department of Commerce, Texas Department of Transportation, the Texas Archives, and the Austin History Center. Many museums, galleries, and chambers of commerce around the state also supplied images, documents, and other information. Finally, much appreciation to my hundreds of former students, who inspired each word; to friends and family; and to all of the many Texans who have gone before us to generate this story about a great and legendary place to live.

Library of Congress Cataloging-in-Publication Data

Turner, Robyn.
    Texas traditions : the culture of the Lone Star state / Robyn Montana Turner.
        p.   cm.
    Includes bibliographical references and index.
    Summary: Discusses the history, geography, industry, and arts of Texas.
    ISBN 0-316-85675-4 (hc).—ISBN 0-316-85639-8 (pb)
    1. Texas—Civilization—Juvenile literature. [1. Texas.]   I. Title.
    F386.3.T87   1996
    976.4—dc20   95-34360

10   9   8   7   6   5   4   3   2   1

S C

Published simultaneously in Canada by Little, Brown & Company (Canada) Limited

Printed in Hong Kong

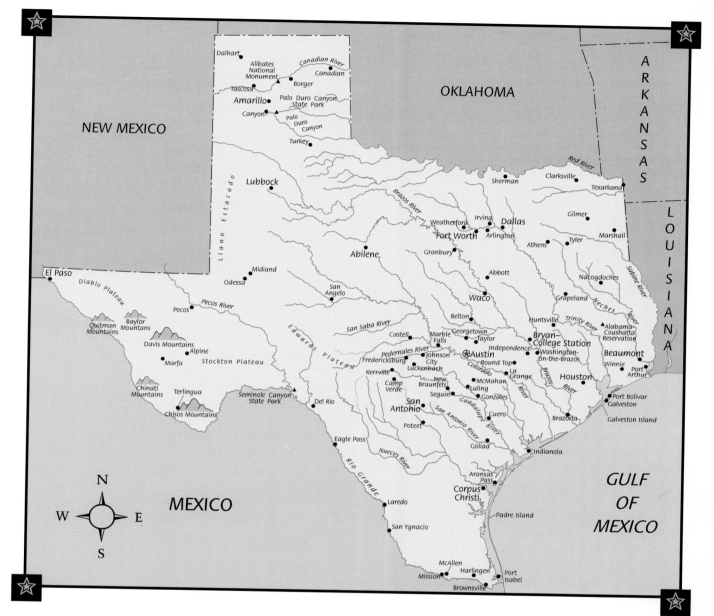

The Geography of *Texas Traditions*

~ · CONTENTS · ~

FOR SALE!
CHOICE OF
300 Half SECTIONS
PREMIUM
Peters' Colony,
OR
Texan Emigration & Land Co.
LANDS
IN THE
Upper Brazos River
COUNTRY;
Selected under an Ex-
clusive Privilege (of 3
years,)—and Patented
over Twenty Years A

A Rich, Beau
and Healthy Country,
not surpassed for Cere
and Stock of all ki
now being Rapidly Settled up
Good Farmers mostly from the
States.

PEACE, Law, Order and Plea
prevails. Crops of every kind of L
Yield and Superior Quality. No Better
Safer Purchase than these Lands, either for Hom
stead or Investment; No better time for Pr
Choice, at Lowest Prices; Nor more than time
est Farms and Ranches in good wording order b
the time several of the Six Railroads Chartered
to pass through this Country will supply the convenience of
rapid travel and cheap freights. Meantime the demands
of the Military Posts West, Immigration, Mining, &c., will
afford ready market at high prices.
Apply to— E. S. GRAHAM.
Graham, Young County, Texas.
Or— J. A. H. HOSACK, Ag't,
At DALLAS and JEFFERSON, TEXAS.
SEPTEMBER, 1872.

First Company of
TEXAN
VOLUNTEERS!
FROM NEW ORLEANS

THE
YELLOW ROSE OF TEXAS
SONG & CHORUS
COMPOSED AND ARRANGED EXPRESSLY FOR
Charles H. Brown
by
J. K.

NEW YORK

CHAPTER ONE

Faces of Texans

Camp of the Lipans, by Theodore Gentilz. Oil on canvas, 9" x 12". Courtesy of the Witte Museum, San Antonio, Texas.

The story of Texas is filled with adventures of people who built a legendary state. The first inhabitants arrived thousands of years ago. Other settlers came more recently from various parts of the United States, Mexico, and other countries. It's no wonder that today's Texans are a people of many cultures.

Every culture carries with it a story of its own rich history. That story reflects the ideas, beliefs, and values of the people who share that culture. It describes their customs, or ways of doing things. Like the threads of a finely woven blanket, the various cultures add beauty and interest to the whole.

Most Texans appreciate the many differences as well as the many similarities among the state's ethnic groups. Members of each ethnic group share a common racial, national, or religious background.

The importance of ethnicity in Texas varies from one person to another. Some Texans feel that cultural traits of their ethnic group are important to their self-image. They identify with the language, food preferences, clothing, religion, and other characteristics of their ethnic group. For others, ethnicity is not central to their daily lives.

The diversity among the faces of Texans, along with the lure of the Lone Star land, have for many years made the state a special place. Texas boasts a rugged and romantic history. It has been home to both indigenous and immigrant people. Today's Texans honor many different traditions as they work together to build a common culture. Del Weniger, a Texas biologist and writer, explains:

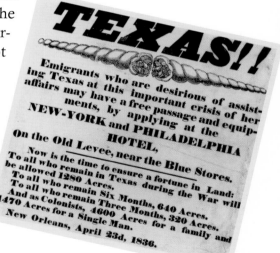

In the beginning, place and people were caught in a delicate, and sometimes not so delicate, balance. From that union the history comes forth. We late-born citizens melt down everything, lump everything together, describe the immense number of changes with one and the same term — Texas.

Native American Texans

Many scientists believe that the first people to set foot in North America came from Asia. They crossed the Bering Strait into what is now called Alaska. They then gradually traveled southward by foot in search of wild animals for food. These Paleo-Indians moved through the Americas about 40,000 years ago. Some groups reached the land now called Texas, about 3,500 miles from where their ancestors may have first crossed over.

Scientists named the first known culture in Texas the Llano culture, which they identified from tools and other relics. It existed 10,000 to 15,000 years ago. Llano people shared a common way of life, moving from place to place hunting giant mammoths and mastodons. Their flint weapons have been found in the western part of Texas, where the flat plains supported big game. Farther north in Texas lived the Folsom people. They hunted giant buffalo, known as bison, between 8,000 and 10,000 years ago.

Sometime after 6000 B.C., the large bison disappeared, possibly because of hunting by humans. For the first time in Texas, people began to gather berries, roots, nuts, and seeds to add to their meals. This dependence on plants for food caused them to

Evidence of the first North American settlers, the Paleo-Indians, has been discovered in Texas. In 1953 the discovery of an 8,000-year-old skeleton, dubbed "Midland Minnie," near Midland made headlines. Almost thirty years later, archaeologists found 10,000-year-old "Leanderthal Lady" near Leander, in Central Texas.

This artist's interpretation of "Midland Minnie" is based on both fact and imagination.

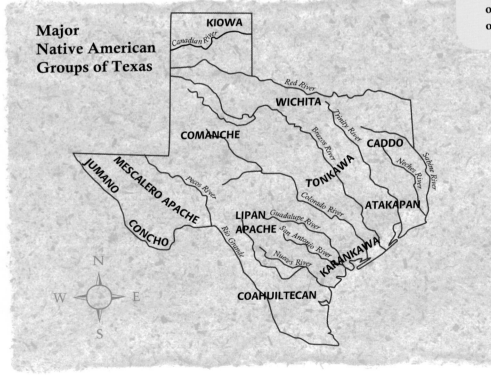

Major Native American Groups of Texas

KIOWA
Canadian River
Red River
WICHITA
Trinity River
COMANCHE
Brazos River
CADDO
Neches River
Sabine River
JUMANO
MESCALERO APACHE
Pecos River
TONKAWA
Colorado River
ATAKAPAN
CONCHO
LIPAN Guadalupe River
APACHE San Antonio River
Rio Grande
KARANKAWA
Nueces River
COAHUILTECAN

N
W E
S

Comanche families such as this one lived on the plains of Texas before reservations were created by the United States government.

settle into more permanent locations so they could grow food.

By 1528, when Europeans first landed on the Texas coast, twelve different cultural groups of Native Americans had made their homes on the land. Most Europeans called these indigenous people Indians, the name Columbus had mistakenly given all Native Americans. Members of each group lived in a special area they had chosen. Each group formed a society.

People in each society spoke the same language. They shared ideas and beliefs about everything from recipes and religion to rules for raising children. Their ways of life were advanced. After all, their ancestors had discovered agriculture, invented the bow and arrow, and made pottery. Each group used the natural resources around them.

As new settlers arrived from Europe and later the United States, the twelve Native American groups didn't survive. Some of them died from diseases brought by the newcomers. Others were killed in battle over land disputes with settlers. In 1854 the United States

Members of one of the twelve Native American groups in Texas gave the state its name. The Caddoes called each other Tayshas, meaning friends or allies. When the Spanish explorers arrived, Caddoes called them Tayshas, too. Soon the explorers began referring to nearby Native Americans who were friendly as Tejas (TAY-hahs). This term was later adapted into English as TEXAS.

government set up the first two reservations in Texas. They "reserved" these sections of land for Native Americans. The reservations were created to stop the conflict over land with the new settlers. By the end of the 1860s, most Native Americans had left Texas or were forced to leave. Many migrated to reservation land in Indian Territory (present-day Oklahoma).

Today many Native American Texans live in cities miles away from the homes of their ancestors. Only the Tiguas, the Alabama-Coushattas, and the Kickapoos live on reservations in Texas.

The native dress of the Tigua group is worn today during special celebrations.

Mexican Texans

Traditional Mexican clothing continues to be worn by both young and old for festive occasions.

Before Texas became a republic and then a part of the United States, it was a part of Mexico. Many people who made Texas their home at that time were of Native American, Spanish, and Mexican cultures.

Early Mexican Texan women and men were called Tejanas and Tejanos. They lived in San Antonio, La Bahía, and Nacogdoches. Many of them farmed and ranched the nearby land. Tejanas took care of family needs, domestic animals, and the garden. Some of them handled the finances for farming or ranching. Others helped organize community events. The Tejanos ran large herds of livestock and managed the vaqueros, the first cowboys, who worked for them.

The Tejanas and Tejanos introduced many customs and habits that are still part of modern-day Texas life. Language is an example. Although English is the primary language of Texas today, Spanish has long been a part of the Texas vocabulary. Terms such as *rodeo, tamale, enchilada, siesta, frijole, piñata, hacienda, rancho, loco,* and *serape* are household words. Both Spanish and English are spoken throughout the state. Many Texans are bilingual, speaking both languages.

Mexicans also introduced ways of doing things. Texas cowboys, for example, learned their trade from Mexican vaqueros. The vaqueros captured the cattle that roamed the dry South Texas plains and began the Texas cattle industry. Many historians believe that the tradition of cattle-branding is of Mexican origin. Some cowboy clothing and equipment originated with the Mexican vaqueros as well. The cowboys' broad-brimmed hat evolved from the large sombrero vaqueros wore. Seatless leather pants, called chaps (pronounced "shaps"), protected cowboys' legs from cactus and thick brush. *Chaps* is short for *chaperejos,* the Spanish word meaning "leather breeches." Spurs for boots were often modeled after Mexican spurs. And Texas cowboys often preferred the Mexican saddle over the European style.

Mexican Texans were also pioneers in the use of irrigation in farming. Other examples of Mexican contributions to Texan

The vaqueros were the first cowboys. This painting shows the traditional dress of an early vaquero.

This young boy sports the dress of the mariachi, or Mexican street band, tradition.

society are types of foods and ways of preparing them, styles of clothing, and architecture.

Today Mexican-American Texans make up about one quarter of the state's population. By 2010 the percentage is expected to rise to almost one third. The Mexican Texans are a strong influence on the evolution of the state.

Henry B. González served as a state senator. In 1961 he was elected to a seat in the United States Congress.

Coronado Entering Palo Duro Canyon, 1541, by Ben Carlton Mead. Courtesy of the Panhandle-Plains Historical Museum Photo Archive.

This mural of Coronado and his men exploring the Palo Duro Canyon is painted on a wall of the Panhandle-Plains Historical Museum.

European Texans

Europeans who settled in Texas came from more than twenty-five countries. Only thirty years after Columbus arrived in the Americas, explorers, gold seekers, and adventurers were leaving Europe for "the New World."

Spain was among the first countries to send explorers to Texas shores. In fact, more than one Texas legend claims that the first Thanksgiving Day was celebrated by Spanish adventurers in Texas. Of course, most historians agree that the first Thanksgiving was celebrated in 1621 at Plymouth Colony, in Massachusetts. However, in 1541 Spanish explorer Francisco Vásquez de Coronado led his troops through Texas's Palo Duro Canyon. There, after weeks of travel in the desert, they

German settler John Meusebach met with twenty Comanche chiefs and signed a treaty. The Comanches allowed the Germans to enter Indian territory unharmed and to settle in the San Saba River area.

Wilhelm and Elise Waerenskjold immigrated from Norway to Texas with their children, Otto and Elise.

*T*he Waerenskjold family came to Texas from Norway during the mid-1800s. As a wife, mother, and community activist, Elise Waerenskjold brought with her many concerns. In a letter dated January 6, 1857, she expresses some of her beliefs about the abuse of alcohol:

Because I hate liquor, it is a great joy to me that Wilhelm never tastes it. He organized a temperance society in our settlement, and since then the community has become so respectable and sober that it is a real pleasure. All of us Norwegians, about eighty persons counting young and old, can come together for a social gathering without having strong drink but we do have coffee, ale, milk, and mead at our gatherings, and food in abundance. . . . Yes, liquor destroys both body and soul.

finally came upon wild fruit and water. Coronado and thirty other men continued their search for gold, while the priest Juan de Padilla stayed with the remaining men to conduct a feast of Thanksgiving.

Both Spain and France later settled parts of the Texas territory. But the largest European migration to Texas happened during the mid-1800s, just after Texas had become a part of the United States. Many people from Germany, Poland, France, Norway, Greece, Italy, Belgium, and other parts of Europe left the crowded cities and set sail for the land of opportunity. Each group brought their cultural habits and customs to the new land. These immigrants spoke a variety of languages. Each group ate different foods. Each had its own ways of doing things.

When their sailing ships arrived on the Texas coast, many of the immigrants walked hundreds of miles to find land to settle. Not everyone survived the weather, the diseases, and the battles with some groups of Native Texans who were upset over land disputes.

*C*aroline von Hinueber was eleven when her family arrived from Germany. According to Caroline's description, their first house looked like a typical house in her homeland:

It was roofed with straw and had six sides, which were made out of moss. The roof was by no means waterproof, and we often held an umbrella over our bed when it rained at night. . . . Of course we suffered a great deal in the winter. My father had tried to build a chimney and fireplace out of logs and clay, but we were afraid to light a fire because of our straw roof. So we had to shiver.

The daughter of a Norwegian immigrant, Port Arthur's Mildred Ella "Babe" Didrikson Zaharias (1912–1956) was perhaps the greatest woman athlete of all time. In 1950 she was named Woman Athlete of the First Half of the Twentieth Century. During her early career, she won medals for events in basketball, baseball, and track and field.

Anglo-American Texans

At the same time that Europeans were arriving in Texas, GTT — "Gone to Texas" — signs appeared on thousands of front doors in Tennessee, Alabama, and other southern states. These signs often were the only remaining traces of life there during the 1800s. Some people were fleeing from the law or from debts. Others were simply searching for a better life. No matter the reason for going, they all set out to claim a plot of land in that huge and vast place called Texas.

Many of these new settlers were Anglo-Americans — Americans of English, Scottish, or Irish ancestry. They traveled by horse, stagecoach, covered wagon, and even by foot. Their journeys were filled with adventure as well as pain.

Just as the European immigrants to Texas had infringed upon Native American territories, so too did the arrival of Anglo-American settlers create land disputes with the indigenous people. During the 1800s, Native American Texans and the new colonists fought many small wars over this issue. Sam Houston, a leader among Anglo-American Texans, befriended many Native Texans and created peace treaties with various indigenous groups. Sadly, he was unable to honor every treaty because of higher rules from the United States government.

As they arrived on the new frontier in East and Central Texas, Anglo-American settlers built several styles of houses. Most of the structures were made of natural resources such as logs and stone. The "dog-run" architectural style was popular with many of these Texas pioneers. An open space separated the two rooms of the log cabin, all covered by a single roof. The "dog-run" construction helped breezes flow

Today in Texas, the expression "GTT" jokingly means that someone won't be back for a while.

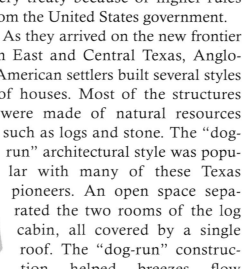

Mary Ann Maverick, a ranch woman, is surrounded by her children in this photograph from the mid-1800s.

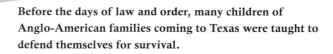

Before the days of law and order, many children of Anglo-American families coming to Texas were taught to defend themselves for survival.

through the cabin during the hot summers. This open space also served as sleeping quarters for guests and the family dogs.

In 1854 Anglo-American settlers Samuel and Mary Ann Maverick established a ranch near San Antonio, where Samuel served as mayor. The Maverick family never got around to branding their cattle, and their strays often wandered into branded herds. Soon the word *maverick* came to refer to unbranded cattle. Today the term is used to refer to someone who acts independently of others.

Anglo and other women of early Texas had a maverick attitude about their position on the new frontier. They worked long and hard every day in their homes. As community volunteers, women started schools, opened libraries, demanded churches, and organized social events. In these ways, those strong pioneers carried the culture. They provided places where ideas, beliefs, and values could be shared. As Sarah T. Hughes, U.S. district court judge from Dallas, describes it:

> Women who came to Texas in the early nineteenth century were ill-prepared for the trials and hardships that awaited them. Courage and determination were as much required of women as of men, and women helped build houses, tended the livestock, and slept on crude beds of logs with rope or rawhide lacings for springs. A gun was always close at hand.

As the nineteenth century moved ahead, many Anglo-American families moved into West Texas to settle. On the flat, dry plains they faced weather extremes and isolation. Establishing a farm required the help of the women and children. Crops took priority over school. Most Texas children were lucky if they attended school often enough to learn reading, writing, and arithmetic. Farm women believed that hard work was the key to success, and they labored from dawn to dusk.

Indeed Texas is a maverick state. The independent spirit of the early Anglo-American colonists lives on today in the attitudes and values of Texans. This rugged independence has produced many leaders, including two United States presidents: Dwight D. Eisenhower and Lyndon Baines Johnson.

Lyndon Baines Johnson (1908–1973)

Who would've known that this lively Texas boy would grow up to become president of the United States? Today LBJ's childhood home in Johnson City is a museum. The LBJ Library and Museum in nearby Austin houses his presidential papers and other keepsakes.

United States President Lyndon Baines Johnson was born in 1908 near Stonewall, in Central Texas. He grew up in nearby Johnson City. His paternal great-granduncle, John Wheeler Bunton, was a six-foot-four-inch Tennesseean. He had come to Texas in 1835, then fought in the Battle of San Jacinto. Bunton became a political leader in the new Republic of Texas.

In 1858 Bunton persuaded his brother, Robert Bunton, to move to Texas. Little did Robert Bunton realize that his own great-grandson would grow up to be a powerful leader.

Like his great-granduncle John, Lyndon Baines Johnson would be tall and lanky, take risks, and become interested in politics. As a young man, Lyndon was elected to the Texas legislature, then the United States Congress, and later the presidency.

African-American Texans

The first known African person to set foot on Texas soil was traveling with the first Europeans to arrive in Texas. Estéban was an enslaved African voyaging by ship with Spanish explorer Alvar Núñez Cabeza de Vaca. The ship wrecked in 1528 near Galveston Island, where the handful of survivors walked ashore to meet the local indigenous people, the Karankawas. Although the Karankawas treated them kindly, they forced Estéban and the Spaniards to live with them for seven years.

One day during their captivity, Cabeza de Vaca removed an arrow from a Karankawa who had been wounded by an enemy. From then on, Estéban, Cabeza de Vaca, and the other Spaniards were thought of as healers, or shamans. They were given more freedom. Finally they escaped to Mexico.

Estéban was considered a healer by Indian Texans.

Later, long before Texas became a part of the United States, free blacks who had come to Texas from other states lived under Spanish rule. During that time, many African Texans were farmers. Others taught school or mined the land. Some worked as merchants or teachers. By 1791 about one fourth of the Texas population had come from Africa.

When Anglo-Americans began to settle in Texas during the early 1800s, some brought enslaved African Americans with them. Slavery was then legal in the United States.

Kiamatia "Kian" Long was a young slave. She belonged to James and Jane Long, Texas settlers from Louisiana. Kian and Jane landed at Port Bolivar in about 1820. For two years they stayed there, waiting for James to return from Mexico. Kian helped Jane with her children and everyday chores. Together they survived bad weather conditions and protected their home against Native Americans who were angry about losing their homelands.

When Jane and Kian learned that James had been killed in Mexico, they moved to Brazoria. There they opened a business offering room and board. Boarders had their own bedroom and ate in a shared dining room. Kian eventually had four children. Her daughter and her granddaughter stayed with the Long family as people in slavery.

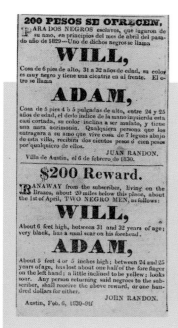

An advertisement about two runaway men in slavery appeared in the *Texas Gazette* in 1830. It was written in both English and Spanish.

These two formerly enslaved African Texans posed for a photograph after they were freed.

Working for no pay and unable to own land, people in slavery had no rights. They were bought and sold as property, often being separated from their families.

The issue of slavery was settled only by the Civil War, during which Texas joined the Confederacy. In 1863 President Abraham Lincoln signed the Emancipation Proclamation, declaring all slaves in the rebelling states free. But the law wouldn't take effect till the war ended, in April 1865. Official word of the law reached Texas on June 19, 1865. Every year since then, Texans have observed the Nineteenth of June, also known as Juneteenth, as a day of celebration.

For the next hundred years, however, African Americans still were not treated fairly. In Texas, as in many southern states, they attended separate schools that were poorly funded. They did not have a choice about where to sit on buses and trains. Most restaurants wouldn't serve them. They had to sit in the balcony at movie theaters. Separate drinking fountains and public restrooms bore the labels "colored" and "white."

During the 1960s, people of other ethnic groups worked alongside blacks to change unfair customs. The Johnson Administration passed federal laws to give African Americans equal rights.

Today African Americans make up about 12 percent of Texas's population. They serve as elected officials, teachers, doctors, business leaders, and in other professions. They bring rich contributions to the culture of Texas in many fields, including music, dance, visual arts, and sports. Through the oral tradition of storytelling, African-American Texans have related their history from one generation to the next.

Barbara Jordan has served Texas as both a state legislator and a congresswoman. She was the first African-American woman from the South to serve in Congress. Today she is a professor at the Lyndon Baines Johnson School of Public Affairs, in Austin.

Asian-American Texans

During the late 1800s, many men sailed from Hong Kong to California, then came to Texas to build the first railroads in the state. They worked hard and kept to themselves as a group.

Sam Mardock arrived from China in 1880 as a railroad worker. Within ten years he had opened a restaurant in Tyler, then five others in nearby towns.

In 1900 Mardock returned to Canton, China, to marry. Many years later, he was finally able to bring his wife to Texas. A large crowd greeted her at the old Cotton Belt Depot in Tyler. She was clothed in her native dress. Her feet were bound, which was a thousand-year-old Chinese custom common then for women and girls. She was happy to be in Texas, where everyone could wear boots or moccasins or even no shoes if they chose. She quickly removed the bindings from her feet.

The Chinese brought their own ways of doing things to the larger Texas culture. For example, Chinese Texans read their books from back to front and sentences from right to left. When they introduced themselves, they said their surname first. Their compass needles pointed south. They even mounted their horses on the right side.

By the time they had completed the railroads, some Chinese men wanted to settle in Texas. Many became successful as owners of small businesses, such as restaurants and laundries. They wished their family members in China could join them. But between 1882 and 1943, the United States government unfortunately allowed few Chinese to enter the country.

After 1943 more Chinese came to the cities of Texas. They quickly adapted to their new environment, while preserving customs of their ancient culture. Many Chinese-American Texans, for example, can read a modern newspaper and a thousand-year-old calligraphy scroll with the same ease. Today Houston has a large Chinese-American community, with Chinese grocery stores, churches, and theaters. Chinese residents even have their own newspaper and celebrate the Chinese Lunar New Year by having a colorful parade.

For many years, Chinese women weren't allowed in Texas. Chinese men built the railroads and only later were permitted to send for their wives.

Like the Chinese, many of the first Japanese people in Texas settled in and near Houston. They lived in tight-knit communities. They grew rice in the flat and wet fields that were level with the sea. In 1908 the Kishi colony harvested 15,753 two-hundred-pound sacks of rice. The crop brought $47,000, a generous sum in 1908. When friends and relatives in Japan heard this news, the colony soon grew.

During the past thirty years, many more Japanese-American families have moved to Texas. Some work in the computer industry or as engineers. Others are landscape artists, musicians, teachers, and business owners. These and other occupations represent only a few of the many contributions of Japanese Texans.

During the last few years of his long life, Isamu Taniguchi (1897–1992) created a beautiful Japanese garden. Then he gave it to the people of Texas. Taniguchi's garden decorates three acres in Zilker Park, a special public gathering place in Austin.

Taniguchi wanted his garden to symbolize world peace. The artist worked with children to show them how a small seed can grow to become a large plant. He demonstrated how the "tools" of his garden work together in a peaceful way. Today a children's gardening group continues to meet in Taniguchi's honor. They call themselves "Sprout Scouts."

The ending of the Vietnam War in 1975 brought other Asian groups to Texas. Refugees from Vietnam, Laos, and Cambodia left their homelands in fear of the new governments. Today most of those Asian-American Texans live in the large cities. Many fish for shrimp along the Texas coast, just as they fished in the waters near their homelands.

Isamu Taniguchi was a Japanese Texan artist with unusual tools. The land was his canvas. His paints were trees, shrubs, ponds, lily pads, beautiful walkways, and stones.

Crossing Cultures

Today many Texans can claim a blend of ethnic origins. Long ago, however, not as many lifestyles crossed cultural boundaries in Texas. Fascinating accounts of early Texans who became closely tied to other cultures have become legendary. Such is the story of Cynthia Ann Parker and her son Quanah.

In 1836 nine-year-old Cynthia Ann Parker, an Anglo-American Texan, was captured by a band of Comanches during a raid on Parker's Fort in present-day Limestone County. The Comanches gave her to one of their families and called her Naduah.

Because Cynthia Ann was so young, she quickly learned the language of the group. In fact, she forgot how to speak or understand English. She grew to feel at home roaming the plains with her new family.

When she was older, she married Peta Nocona, who later became chief. Their children, Quanah, Pecos, and Prairie Flower, appeared more Indian than Anglo, and they learned the Comanche ways of doing things.

Twenty-four years after the Comanche raid, Cynthia Ann and Prairie Flower became captives of Texas Rangers, law officers who patrolled the Texas frontier. Colonel Isaac Parker, Cynthia Ann's uncle, identified her as his long-lost niece. Her uncle said the names of her relatives, but she did not respond. Just as he was about to give up, Cynthia Ann sadly muttered, "Me, Cincee Ann." Then from her mouth spilled a string of Comanche words. An interpreter explained that she described the raid on Parker's Fort and her Comanche family.

In 1864 Cynthia Ann Parker died of the same fever that had claimed Prairie Flower only months before. The legendary woman never knew what became of her husband and two sons.

In fact, Nocona died three or four years after Cynthia Ann's capture by the Rangers, and Pecos died before he reached manhood. Quanah, her oldest son, learned of his mother's fate in 1867. He had never forgotten her and took her surname as his own. Otherwise, only his blue eyes revealed his Anglo heritage.

Quanah Parker became chief of the Quahadi band of the Comanches. He helped his people reach agreements with the United States government. Both Indians and Anglos respected him for they knew he wanted peace between the two cultures.

Six Flags Over Texas

Although many more than six flags have flown over the land we now call Texas, six of the more familiar flags continue to fly today in several Texas cities. They are the flags of the six nations of which Texas has been a part during its almost five hundred years of recorded history. Today, as a reminder of their love for the state, Texans often fly the Lone Star flag beneath Old Glory.

Spain 1519–1821

Texas Republic 1836–1845

France 1685–1690

Confederacy 1861–1865

Mexico 1821–1836

United States of America
1845–1861; 1865–present

How Texas Got Its Lone Star

On June 24, 1934, an article by T. B. Baldwin appeared in the *Dallas News*, discussing how Texas got its Lone Star. His account describes the actions of Henry Smith, who in 1821 became the first governor of the Mexican Province of Texas— and reportedly gave Texas its Lone Star, which is a part of the official state seal.

In Smith's day overcoats had large brass buttons. It happened that the buttons on the coat of Governor Smith had the impress of a five-pointed star. A few days after he was inaugurated Governor, a messenger arrived with important papers. After reading and signing them the Governor said: "Texas should have a seal," and forthwith he cut one of the big buttons from his overcoat and with sealing wax stamped the impress of the Lone Star upon the documents.

CHAPTER TWO

The Call of the Land

Enchanted Rock (Scene near Fredericksburg), by Hermann Lungkwitz. Oil on canvas, 14" x 20". Courtesy of the Witte Museum, San Antonio, Texas.

Gary P. Nunn, a Texas songwriter, sings about the call of the land in "What I Like About Texas." His lyrics describe the physical and cultural beauty of the state:

You ask me what I like about Texas.
I tell you it's the wide-open spaces.
Everything between the Sabine and the Rio Grande.
It's the Llano Estacado.
It's the Brazos and the Colorado.
It's the spirit of the people who share this land.

As the song reveals, the land called Texas allures, enchants, and captivates. Throughout the centuries it has influenced the way Texans live. Its fertile soil and rivers have nourished them, while its weather conditions have sometimes challenged their very existence.

The first Texas cultures were closely tied to the land. Each group used the plants, animals, and other natural resources in different ways. Some people stayed in one place and developed the land around them. Others traveled to hunt wild game. Still others crossed borders to trade their goods.

In 1824, when Texas belonged to Mexico, Mexican law had rules that protected new landowners. These rules encouraged settlement of the Texas territory by anyone who would become a citizen of Mexico. Word quickly spread, and people flocked to Coahuila y Tejas, as Texas was then called.

As the 1800s marched on, Texans discovered new ways to develop the land, making plants and animals important to the economic system. Cotton became "king" in Texas and in other southern states. Cowboys drove cattle from the Midwest of the United States through Texas.

During the 1900s, the land's natural resources have continued to draw people from all walks of life. Some of them have traveled from across the world to make their homes in the Lone Star State. Others have had only to cross a border. New Mexico, Oklahoma, Arkansas, Louisiana, and Mexico have had a special impact on the culture of Texas because they share its borders.

The mighty Rio Grande connects Mexico with the United States at the Texas border.

Land Meets Water

Texas claims not only land as its border but a river and a gulf as well. These water borders affect the culture of the surrounding communities.

The longest river in the state is the Rio Grande. It forms an international boundary between the United States and Mexico and extends 1,270 miles along Texas.

Cross the Rio Grande at any of the border towns along its course and step into another country. Suddenly the aromas of sizzling fajitas, squash blossom quesadillas, and sweet cactus candy fill the air. The vibrant colors and patterns of fabrics, baskets, and pottery decorate the *mercados,* or marketplaces. *Conjunto* music vibrates from storefronts. Since the passage of NAFTA, the North American Free Trade Agreement, in 1993, Texas has become a gateway to trade among the North American countries. NAFTA was crafted to provide greater opportunities for Canada, the United States, and Mexico. Each day, many goods cross the Rio Grande on bridges along the border towns, where cultures meet.

People of all ages love to play on Texas's beaches along the Gulf of Mexico.

The Texas coastline on the Gulf of Mexico wraps around the southeastern border of the state. This large body of water provides a livelihood for shrimpers and fishers. Its moisture creates a good climate for growing rice and other crops on the nearby wetlands. The Gulf serves as a highway for ships that transport goods to and from Texas ports. It's home to a fascinating family of aquatic plants and animals. Some of them are endangered or threatened species that need protection. This 450-mile Texas border also provides sandy beaches, where people play and relax.

Wind and Weather

The warm, sunny climate makes Texas a desirable place to live most of the time. "Can't blame it on the weather" is a typical greeting on a Texas afternoon.

On the other hand, the state has its share of damaging weather. As another saying goes, "If you don't like the weather in Texas, stick around five minutes, and it'll change." Hurricanes rip through coastal communities. Tornadoes flatten entire towns. Blue northers chill the Panhandle ranch lands. A popular Texas joke goes so far as to say, "When Noah built the ark and it rained for forty days and nights, West Texas got half an inch." And yet the people in Texas thrive. It seems as though severe weather toughens their spirits.

During the 1930s, a major drought hit the Texas plains. Farmers had replaced the natural vegetation with wheat crops, so the soil was without roots to secure it between harvesting and planting time. Few trees grew on the plains as wind barriers, so the winds gathered strength as they swept across the land. They picked up the top layer of loose soil and stirred it into what became known as the Dust Bowl.

While Texans endured the Dust Bowl, they gave thanks for their windmills. These wooden towers tapped underground water supplies for crop irrigation, livestock, and household use. Ranchers and farmers no longer had to depend upon lakes, ponds, and rivers for water.

Today steel windmills have all but taken the place of the old wooden ones. In addition, another type of windmill called a wind generator or wind turbine can been spotted in parts of West Texas. These eighty-foot towers, each with three giant blades, generate electricity from breezes as slow as nine miles an hour. They offer clean and renewable energy. In these and other ways, the winds of Texas could someday supply about 10 percent of the nation's electric power.

Texans base many recreational activities on the weather. Many of them plan their livelihoods around it. It can even affect their moods. The food they eat is a product of weather. They talk about the weather, sing about it, and write about it.

The thickness of the dust blown up by winds across the Dust Bowl made an otherwise sunny day appear pitch black. That's the sight Pauline Durrett Robertson of Amarillo, Texas, witnessed at age thirteen. She and a friend were outside playing as the dark cloud approached:

We were running away from it and toward home when the wind hit, pelting our bare legs with gravel. We choked and gasped and ran as the air thickened with brown dust. . . . Just as we reached my front porch everything went completely black. The porchlight was consumed by the blackness. We couldn't see each other's faces. We couldn't see our own hands. I remember gasping, 'I can't breathe!'

In 1900, the Great Galveston storm hit Texas, becoming the worst natural disaster to that date in United States history. Hurricane tides reaching fifteen feet or more drowned 6,000 to 8,000 people.

Landmarks

Every state has its landmarks — telltale stones or trees, historic buildings, significant hills, or other geographic features associated with legend or fact. Landmarks are symbols of regional lore that help define the culture of an area. Texas has an abundance of these monuments — from the Alamo to Alibates.

"Remember the Alamo!" can be heard even today about the best-known historic shrine in Texas. The slogan originated with determined Texans. In 1836 they vowed to conquer the Mexican army after its bitter victory at the dramatic Battle of the Alamo.

But that same Alamo mission, which stands today in downtown San Antonio, is a reminder of many events and people in Texas history. For example, it represents the cultures of Indian Texans and Spanish priests, who built the limestone and adobe structure in 1718. Mission San Antonio de Valero, as it was then called, was their school, home, and place of worship.

Alibates Flint Quarries is Texas's only national monument. In 1930 scientists realized that the flint from this ten-square-mile area in

The historic Alamo mission is a landmark in modern-day downtown San Antonio. The word *alamo* means cottonwood in Spanish. The mission was possibly named for a grove of nearby cottonwood trees.

This arrowhead is made of flint from the Alibates Flint Quarries National Monument in the Panhandle of Texas.

Two Lighthouse Landmarks

The word *lighthouse* has at least two meanings in Texas. At the southern tip of the state, the beacon at Port Isabel shines its warning light across the night waters as it welcomes ships ashore. Some 750 miles north, another "lighthouse," a three-hundred-foot-tall rock formation, welcomes wildlife and rugged hikers to the heart of the Palo Duro Canyon State Park.

the Texas Panhandle had been mined by Native Americans at least 12,000 years ago. Spear points made of Alibates flint were found in or near skeletons of ancient mammoths and buffalo.

Later, about 1000 to 1450 A.D., Indian Texans in the Panhandle traded the blanks, or chunks of flint, to be made into tools in many parts of North America. In exchange they received goods such as painted pottery, shells, turquoise, and red pipestone.

No one would have been more surprised than the old cowboy Allie Bates to find that Texas's only national monument carries an adaptation of his name. In 1903 geology professor Charles Newton Gould mapped the

Another Texas landmark is *Big Tex,* a fifty-two-foot-tall sculpture made of iron-pipe drill casing and papier-mâché. He took up residence at the Texas State Fair in Dallas in 1952. Before that, he was a giant Santa Claus.

area. He tried to label the geographic features with names that area residents had already chosen. Since Allie Bates lived in a dugout shelter along a dry creek bed, people told Gould to call the creek Allie Bates Creek.

In 1907 Gould then discovered the dolomite flint quarries that Native Texans had known for more than 10,000 years. Since geological sites are generally named for the nearest recognized geographic feature, Gould used "Alibates," a shortened term for Allie Bates Creek. In 1965, when the United States Congress declared the Alibates Flint Quarries a national monument for its significance as an ancient Native American mining site, Allie Bates had long since disappeared. No one knows if he ever heard that his name had become nationally known.

Texas Flora

Differences in climate, soil, and elevation create various growing conditions across Texas. Plant life responds to those conditions. This is why Texas has so many types of trees, grasses, flowers, and other forms of vegetation. They affect the ways people live.

Natural Vegetation —

Wildflowers, brush, trees, bushes, native grasses, and other wild plants are types of natural vegetation in Texas. They grow without assistance from people. These plants prevent erosion, provide food for animals, and beautify the Texas landscape.

The heavy rains in the eastern third of Texas encourage forest plants to grow. From the fertile soil sprout trees, tall grasses, and bushes. Beautiful loblolly pine trees fill the Piney Woods. Other trees common to East Texas are elm, hickory, dogwood, and oak.

Along the humid and tropical Gulf coast of South Texas, palm trees and blossoming flowers decorate the landscape. Grasses cover the dry plains of South Texas. Mesquite trees compete for space with cacti and shrubs. In

Primrose Path, by Susan M. Mayer

The bluebonnet was adopted March 7, 1901, as the state flower. Several varieties of this Texas wildflower grow throughout the state. This one is found in Central Texas. As in all varieties, each bonnet faces the stem. A legend about the bluebonnet can be found on page 37.

South Texas wildflowers, including Indian paintbrush and yucca blossoms, brighten the landscape during the spring months.

White dogwood blossoms of East Texas provide unexpected highlights in the forests at night.

Central Texas, the pecan tree thrives beside rivers and in neighborhood yards and parks. Each fall the fruit of the official state tree becomes filling for holiday pies.

Far West Texas is so dry that only plants requiring small amounts of water can survive. Short grasses, cacti, and yucca dot the prairies. As in other areas of Texas, the state grass, sideoats grama, thrives on this arid land. It's a richly nutritious source of food for cattle and sheep. The nearby mountains are home to coniferous, or cone-bearing, trees such as ponderosa pines, piñon pines, and junipers.

The first Texans depended on indigenous, or native, plants for their survival. Texas Indians picked wild berries, nuts, and fruits to eat. From the yucca plant they made shampoos, soaps, and medicines. They harvested wild herbs that fight bacteria. From tree bark they made aspirin-like extracts. The cottonwood tree provided good fuel. The early Texans even made points for bird-hunting arrows from the thorns of the prickly pear cactus.

Through the years, many Texas cultures have concocted their own cure-alls, or folk remedies. The Cherokees swore that a boiling solution of burrs would cure forgetfulness, since "nothing sticks like a burr." Early pioneers often treated aches, pains, and sniffles by drinking a cup of herbal tea. Babies who wouldn't drink mother's milk were given pecan leaf tea. Bandages for wounds were made of clean spiderwebs mixed with a native flower.

Today many Texans continue to enjoy harvesting wild berries, nuts, and fruits. They still use herbs, roots, wildflower blossoms, and other forms of naturally occurring plant life to help cure ailments and prevent illnesses. They are careful in making selections, however, as some native plants can be harmful to human beings.

Claudia Taylor "Lady Bird" Johnson, widow of former president Lyndon Johnson, made a commitment to the nation that would honor its flora. During her husband's presidency, she set about to preserve the wildflowers of America.

After LBJ retired from public office in 1969, Ms. Johnson focused her attention toward Texas. In 1982 she established the National Wildflower Research Center near Austin. Today, her newer center—even bigger and better—in Austin helps people across the country understand the benefits of planting and preserving wildflowers. These natural plants save water, require no chemical fertilizers to thrive, reduce soil erosion, and help maintain the balance of nature.

Although Texas has always had fields of wildflowers, the center's efforts have richly brightened the state's landscape. Each spring many barren Texas prairies are set ablaze with colorful bluebonnets, Indian paintbrush, and Mexican hat. Thanks to the former First Lady, blankets of wildflowers now flank the Texas highways, too.

Cultivated Vegetation —

Plants grown by people for food, fiber, or timber are called cultivated, or domestic, plants. Wheat, cotton, rice, corn, and grain sorghum are the major crops grown across the state. They provide nourishment for many Americans.

Some early Texas Indian groups were agricultural. They stayed in one place and farmed the land. Women did most of the cultivating, while men hunted. These early Texans grew maize (corn), beans, squashes, pumpkins, and sunflowers. Each season they struggled with the devastating effects of droughts and grasshoppers. Their tools were simple. For example, they made hoes from shoulder blades of buffalo. In spite of setbacks, their crops grew well.

When the new settlers arrived, Native American Texans taught some of them how to work the land. Others used their own experience to guide them. Again, women took charge of the family garden. The southern climate proved to be just right for growing fig and peach trees. Garden potatoes, peas, carrots, celery, cabbages, radishes, lettuces, and onions filled the supper tables of early Texas families.

Texas ruby red grapefruit, a South Texas cash crop, is rich in Vitamin C.

The climate in northeastern Texas is ideal for growing roses. Established in 1847, Tyler is known as the rose capital of America. The area's sandy soil, long growing season, and consistent rainfall combine to nourish the world's largest municipal rose garden.

A Pioneer Gardener

Mary Austin Holley, cousin of Stephen F. Austin, first saw Texas in 1831. After traveling throughout the United States, she settled in Brazoria in 1835. She brought with her cuttings of plants she'd collected in her travels to cultivate in her new garden. Within no time, she was able to eat strawberries from the vines she had grown and enjoy the fragrance of the beautiful roses that surrounded her porch.

For more than a century "king cotton" has been a major crop in Texas. Today the Texas cotton harvest amounts to about one third of the total cotton production in the United States.

Texas Fauna

Animals of Yesteryear ﹣

Just as the flora of Texas is interwoven with Texan ways of life, so too is fauna, or animal life, a part of the culture. Texas is known for the many untamed animals that roam its prairies, canyons, hills, mountains, woodlands, and wetlands, as well as the waters of the Gulf. Early Texans often depended upon these animals for food and sometimes for skins. Later, as farmers and ranchers domesticated animals, cattle and sheep helped boost the economy.

It's hard to imagine today's Texas landscape with buffalo and mustang horses roaming wild. Indeed, for many years herds of both wandered over the fenceless Great Plains. At one point, more than a century ago, even camels could be found in Texas!

From 1856 to 1866, the United States Army tried a camel experiment in Texas. The secretary of war, Jefferson Davis, thought camels would provide safe, rapid, and inexpensive transportation in the dry climate of West Texas. He knew that camels could travel thirty

Wild Mustang Horses

This sculpture of wild mustang horses stands in front of the Texas Memorial Museum in Austin. These wild horses took their name from the Spanish word *mestengo* or *mesteño,* meaning stray animal or wild steer. The full-grown mustang horse wasn't large, averaging fourteen hands high. It weighed about seven hundred pounds and was quite fast.

The first horses in North America were brought by Spanish settlers. Native Americans living in Texas and throughout the Southwest adopted horses into their culture and rode them to hunt buffalo. Some of their horses escaped and formed wild herds. These were the first mustangs.

Later, when colonists arrived in Texas, their hunger sometimes led them to eat wild mustangs. During the beginning of the Texas cattle industry, mustangers worked for large cattle outfits and caught the wild horses roaming the Great Plains.

miles per day and carry 450 to 600 pounds. Their upkeep was less than one half that of a mule.

When the first boatload of thirty-four camels landed at Indianola in 1856, onlookers hated the horrible smell. The stubborn camels even spit on some of them! Finally they were herded to Camp Verde, sixty miles northwest of San Antonio. By 1861 the camp had eighty camels and two Egyptian drivers to help corral them. Even so, the experiment failed because only one leader, Jeff Davis, supported the idea. Everyone else was resistant to change. They wanted to return to the days of the horse and mule. The camels were sold for thirty-one dollars each to freight companies in Arizona and California.

Buffalo graze today at the LBJ State Park near Johnson City. Unlike the buffalo of early Texas days, these animals live in a fenced pasture. By the 1880s, Anglo-American buffalo hunters with rifles had killed most of the buffalo in Texas. They sold the hides for clothing in the eastern United States and the meat to feed crews building railroads in the Midwest.

Horny Toad, by James Marsh

Animals of the Wild —

Texas is home to a broad array of wild animals, from the elegant whooping crane to the lumbering armadillo. Since 1973 Texas has legally protected some types of animals, helping to ensure that their species won't disappear. Those species that are close to extinction statewide are called endangered. Threatened species are those that are likely to become endangered in the future. Some plants are endangered or threatened as well.

Horned lizards, or "horny toads," used to live in practically every area of Texas. Now they've disappeared from East Texas and parts of South Texas. Two of the three species of horned lizards are considered threatened. It is thought that too many people have taken them from the wild to keep as pets or that herbicides have killed them. For several years they were even sold in curio stores, which may have contributed to their dwindling population.

High-Tech Horny Toads

In 1994, twenty Texas horned lizards carried tiny backpacks equipped with radio beacons the size of a fingernail. Scientists tracked them across a two-hundred-acre area to learn about where a horned lizard likes to eat, sleep, and habitate. The scientists picked up signals from a three-inch wire antenna. Batteries lasted about seven months. Each lizard was assigned a different radio frequency to make tracking easier. The radio couldn't be attached to the skin because horned lizards shed their skins. Without harming the animals, scientists secured the packs behind the horns and in front of the back legs. Scientists learned that horned lizards can travel several hundred yards each day. They usually roam within a three- to five-acre area, coming back at night to where they started.

WARNING: The Texas horned lizard is a threatened species. It may not be taken, possessed, transported, exported, sold, or offered for sale.

The mockingbird is the state bird of Texas.

The official state mascot, the armadillo, finds food through its sense of smell.

A Texas endangered species, the whooping crane, nests along the Gulf coast.

Whooping Crane, by John James Audubon (1785–1851). Engraving with aquatint (hand-colored), 38 1/8" x 25 1/4". Stark Museum of Art, Orange, Texas.

The armadillo and the Texas cockroach have been around since prehistoric times. The "dillo" doesn't see or hear well, but its sense of smell is keen. It roots around in the soil with its long nose in search of worms to eat. When it moves around, the heavily armored mammal makes as much noise as a frightened deer in the woods. It can travel about as fast as most people can run. Sadly, poor hearing and sight lead many armadillos to their deaths on Texas highways.

The Turtle Lady, as Ila Loetscher is known, has become internationally recognized for her work with threatened and endangered sea turtles. Loetscher works on South Padre Island, where many of the turtles nest.

¡La Cucaracha!

The saying goes that everything in Texas is longer, higher, wider, deeper, taller, and bigger. The cockroach in Central and South Texas is no exception. It is huge — about as big as a grown person's thumb.

Like cockroaches in other parts of the world, this insect's ancestors were important on Earth as long as 280 million years ago. The large brownish-red critter has a flattened, slippery body covered with a shiny, leathery coat. Its six long legs are armed with bristles. Two long antennae, or feelers, help it find its way into just about any situation.

The cockroach typically stays outside beneath stones and leaves or under the bark of rotting trees. At night, however, many roaches slip through cracks in walls to look for something to eat — food, garbage, clothing, bookbindings, furniture — they're not picky.

Just about every Texan has had to devise ways to discourage the varmints from setting up housekeeping in the kitchen. "La Cucaracha," a popular folk song in honor of the critter, keeps Texans smiling about the ongoing challenge.

Animals for Agriculture —

Like cultivated plants, many animals are valuable to the agriculture of the state. Hogs and pigs, chickens, turkeys, and other "barnyard" animals have provided food and trade since the arrival of the first settlers. Cattle and sheep have grazed Texas ranches for more than two hundred years.

Spanish and Mexican ranches in Texas date back to the 1700s. Even before Texas became a state in 1845, energetic colonists rounded up hundreds of thousands of wild cattle to form ranches. They bred their own sheep with Mexican sheep. At that time, most livestock was raised for food and hides.

By the time of the Civil War, Texans were trading sheep and cattle for other goods and for money. These animals provided a livelihood for many people.

Today cattle and sheep continue to be valued resources for the Texas economy. In addition to the meat, cowhides and sheep wool are useful by-products.

This gate sign identifies a Texas ranch.

The Texas longhorn has become a symbol of the Lone Star State. It's sometimes called the cactus boomer, mossy horn, Spanish cow, sea lion, or coaster.

CATTLE WANTED.
I HAVE four leagues of land on *Los Pintos* Creek, in Nueces County, fourteen miles from San Patricio, of the finest grazing qualities, the mes- quit grass being knee high the year round, one-half of which tract I am willing to exchange for stock cattle, and would be willing to make an arrange- ment with the purchaser to place an equal number of cattle on the place, to be placed in charge of a competent American family, and the requisite number of Mexican vaqueros.
Those having large stocks of cattle, would do well to communicate with me. Address me at this place.
WM. H. HOUSTON.
City of Austin, May 31st, 1855.

Sheep ranches have been a part of the Texas culture since the 1700s. Today 20 percent of the wool produced in the United States comes from Texan sheep.

36

The Legend of the State Flower

Long ago in Texas, Comanche dancers called upon the Great Spirits to help them. Winter was over, yet no rains had come from the sky to feed the crops. Plants and animals were dying from the drought. Some Comanches were losing their lives on the hot, dry land. So the Comanche dancers danced. Drummers drummed, and the shaman stood on the mountaintop. Everyone waited for healing rains.

Girl-of-the-Blue-Feather held a doll in her lap. She loved the doll with its beaded buckskin robe. The bright blue feathers in its headdress had been taken from the blue jay.

The girl told the doll not to worry. She stroked the blue headdress, remembering that her father had given her the feathers. Then she looked into the doll's eyes, made of ancient seashells. She cried softly and wished the famine hadn't taken away her parents.

Suddenly the shaman came running down the mountainside. The Great Spirits had spoken. The shaman explained that for too long the people had stolen resources from the earth. Now they must give back a special offering.

The people thought of valuable possessions they could give up to make the drought go away. A corn grinder, bow and arrow, buffalo hide, turquoise ring — each was considered special.

When everyone had gone to sleep, the young Comanche girl took a glowing stick from the campfire. She carried it with the doll to the top of the hill, where the stars lit the sky. She held the doll up to the heavens. Then she told the Great Spirits that the doll was her most special gift because it was the only reminder of her parents.

The girl gathered twigs and with her glowing stick built a fire. Before she could change her mind, she tossed the doll into the flames. For many hours, Girl-of-the-Blue-Feather watched the flames rise up, dance, and flicker until they turned to ashes. When they cooled, she scattered them to the four winds and fell asleep.

When the sun rose, Girl-of-the-Blue-Feather could hardly believe her eyes. Where the ashes had fallen, fields of beautiful bright blue flowers popped up from green grass that now covered the hills. She remembered the bright blue feathers that had decorated the doll's headdress. She thought of her mother and father.

Suddenly the sky cracked wide open, and the rains came pouring down. The people of the Comanche group walked up the hill in the rain. Girl-of-the-Blue-Feather and her people sang and danced all day.

Each spring, rains come to the land now called Texas. Covering the rolling hills and desert countryside, beautiful wildflowers — as blue as a blue jay feather and shaped like bonnets — blossom in the rain.

Legends from various Texas cultures surround the origins of the Texas state flower, sometimes known as lupine, wolf flower, buffalo clover, or *el conejo,* or jackrabbit. This wild lupine received its common name, bluebonnet, when white settlers came to Texas. The formation of the petals reminded settlers of the bonnets worn by women to protect them from the hot Texas sun. The bluebonnet has been the state flower since 1901.

CHAPTER THREE
⋅ ★ ⋅ Lone Star Legacy

Evening Star No. VI, by Georgia O'Keeffe, 1917. Watercolor. Private Collection. Copyright 1995 The Georgia O'Keeffe Foundation/Artists Rights Society (ARS), New York. Photo by Malcolm Varon, N.Y.C. © 1995.

During her years as an art teacher in the Texas Panhandle, Georgia O'Keeffe took many long walks, often at sunset, to observe, think, and imagine. She felt a kinship with the wide-open spaces. In the painting at left, she shows the first evening star — the lone star — shining in the Texas sky.

It's easy to understand why so many people have claimed the land called Texas as their own. They have appreciated its vast size and diverse terrain. They have believed it's a special place to live. They have valued its beauty, its resources, and its people. Ideas, beliefs, and values — these are the stitches that hold together a cultural quilt.

Texans take pride in their state government partly because of its revolutionary beginnings as a separate country. The story of how the early settlers gained their independence from Mexico stands today as a cultural symbol of strength. It represents a time when Texans stood by their ideas, beliefs, and values to protect their way of life. Sadly, thousands of people — both Texans and Mexicans — lost their lives fighting about which government would rule the land. Their disputes were resolved only through war.

For many years, Texans have held a strong belief that educating the state's citizens helps to resolve problems peacefully. They have set up state and local systems of education to teach about ideas and beliefs. Many families and cultural groups support the public school curriculum, adding traditions and values of their own to their children's education.

From the early Texans to those of modern times, many decisions have been based on religious beliefs. Just as ethnicity and language have differed among Texans, so too have religions. People have brought their spiritual practices to Texas from all parts of the world.

Government, education, language, and religion all reflect ways of thinking and believing. Together they form the fabric of the Texan culture.

In 1916 artist Georgia O'Keeffe described these two Texas scenes in letters to her friend Anita Pollitzer:

Tonight I walked into the sunset — to mail some letters — the whole sky — and there is so much of it out here — was just blazing — and grey blue clouds were rioting all through the hotness of it. . . .

Last night I couldn't sleep till after four in the morning — I had been out to the canyon all afternoon — till late at night — wonderful color — I wish I could tell you how big — and with the night the colors deeper and darker — cattle on the pastures in the bottom looked like little pin heads. . . .

Are you for or against Texas' Annexation.
READ AND CIRCULATE!

FREEMEN OF TEXAS
To Arms!!! To Arms!!!!
"Now's the day, & now's the hour."

The Rise of the Lone Star State

Early Texas settlers from the United States came with the belief that their culture would remain about the same, even though they would be citizens of Mexico. As their numbers grew, the influence of the United States became stronger in Texas. For example, the settlers continued to buy many of their goods from the United States rather than from Mexico.

By 1830 Mexico felt threatened by the many new ideas, beliefs, and values that were entering Texas from the United States. The Mexican government feared the United States might try to take over Coahuila y Tejas, as Texas was then called. Mexico began to take steps to discourage Texans from interacting with the United States. These steps marked the beginnings of a cultural clash that would change the history of Texas, Mexico, and the United States.

First, Mexico ended all immigration from the United States. Then, to boost trade with Mexico, it set up a tax for goods coming to Texas from the United States. These laws angered many new settlers, who wanted their relatives to join them. They also feared that the Texas economy would suffer.

Conflicts began to arise between the settlers and Mexican troops. Both sides valued the land so much that lives were lost in scattered battles. Stephen F. Austin, known as the Father of Texas, believed in solving problems through discussion. He tried to

Soldiers of many ethnic origins joined the Texans and Tejanos to fight Santa Anna's army. Hendrick Arnold and Greenberry Logan (above) were among those singled out for their heroic contributions.

Antonio López de Santa Anna ruled Mexico as a dictator during the Texas Revolution.

Lorenzo de Zavala, a native of Mexico, served Santa Anna as a government official before turning against the dictator and moving to Texas. He then joined the Texas convention and became vice president of the new provisional government.

negotiate peace with the Mexican government. But he became frustrated with Santa Anna and other Mexican government officials.

In 1833 Austin wrote a letter to a group of settlers who were organizing to form a convention. They were determined to discuss with each other their ideas, beliefs, and values toward changing the Texas government. In the letter Austin encouraged them to create a separate state government without waiting for permission from Mexican officials. When Mexico's leader, Santa Anna, found out about the letter, he ordered his soldiers to imprison Austin in Mexico for a year.

Even though Santa Anna soon decided to readmit United States citizens to Texas, the trust between the settlers and the Mexican government had been destroyed. They didn't value his word.

Santa Anna had become a military dictator, holding enormous power in the Mexican government. He hadn't allowed the Texans to form a state government separate from Coahuila y Tejas. He hadn't provided enough troops to protect the colonists from Native American raids. He had sent his armies to fight the settlers, who had teamed with Tejanos to revolt against the Mexican government. These teams had defeated Santa Anna's army at Gonzales, Goliad, and San Antonio. Now, during the winter of 1836, Santa Anna's troops were headed for yet another battle with the Texans. This time they would fight at an old Spanish mission, the Alamo, in San Antonio.

Meanwhile fifty-nine Texas delegates who'd received Austin's letter held their convention in a building that belonged to a blacksmith in the small community of Washington-on-the Brazos. The delegates' goal was to write and approve the Texas Declaration of Independence. This document would set the colonists apart from the Mexican government. The Texas Declaration of Independence was adopted on March 2, 1836. That special event is now celebrated every March 2 as Texas Independence Day.

The delegates at Washington-on-the-Brazos listened to one another's ideas and beliefs as the Declaration of Independence was being created.

March 2, 1836	March 6, 1836	April 21, 1836	1839	1840	1842	1845
Texas Declaration of Independence written at Washington-on-the-Brazos.	Mexicans victorious at Battle of the Alamo.	Mexicans surrender to Texans at Battle of San Jacinto.	Waterloo (Austin) becomes Texas state capital. State flag is adopted.	Congress of Texas passes education acts.	Archives War in Austin	Texas gains statehood.

The Fall of the Alamo —

The delegates at the convention were so busy, they didn't have time to keep a written account of the happenings at Washington-on-the-Brazos. However, William F. Gray from Virginia was a visitor to the Constitutional Convention. He kept a diary of his thoughts and beliefs about the historic event.

Sunday, February 28, 1836
Cold and drizzling.
This evening a number of members arrived, among them Lorenzo de Zavala, the most interesting man in Texas. He is a native of Yucatán, Mexico, was governor of a state in Mexico five years, minister of the treasury department, and ambassador to France. He now lives on his estate on Buffalo Bayou, near Galveston Bay.

Tuesday, March 1, 1836
In spite of the cold, the members of the Convention met today in an unfinished house, without doors or window glass. Cotton cloth was stretched across the windows, which partially excluded the cold wind.

Mr. [George C.] Childress from the committee reported a Declaration of Independence. It was received by the house and unanimously adopted in less than one hour from its first and only reading. It underwent no changes. The only speech made upon it was a short address by General Sam Houston.

There being no printing press here, various copies of the Declaration were ordered to be made and sent by express to various points and to the United States for publication.

A committee of one member from each town was appointed to draft a Constitution. They divided themselves into three committees, one for the executive, one for the legislative, and one for the judicial branch. Zavala was chairman of the executive committee.

Friday, March 4, 1836
Today several important committees have been appointed, for example, on finances and on the army, and the Convention adjourned until Monday to give time for the committees to act.

Sam Houston appointed Commander in Chief of the armies.

Sunday, March 6, 1836
This morning, while at breakfast, a dispatch was received from [Colonel William B.] Travis, dated Alamo, March 3, 1836. The members of the Convention and the citizens all crowded into the Convention room to hear it read.

A great many persons are preparing to start to the scenes of fighting. In the afternoon Houston left, accompanied by his staff. The town has been in a bustle all day, but is now quiet enough.

Thursday, March 10, 1836
Fine weather, and we have got comfortably fixed in our new lodging. The eating at our house is becoming sorry — no butter, no milk, no sugar, little or no vegetables, and not much meat except pork.

The business of the Convention moves slowly. The Constitution is a good one, on the whole.

No news yet from the Alamo, and much anxiety is felt for the fate of the brave men there. It is obvious that they must be surrounded and all communication with them cut off.

Tuesday, March 15, 1836
In the afternoon, while the Convention was sitting, a Mr. Ainsworth from Columbia brought news that an express rider had arrived with the intelligence that an attack had been made on the Alamo, which was repulsed with great loss to the enemy. The rumor was doubted but all hoped it true. But many feared the worst. Half an hour later an express was received from General Sam Houston, bringing the sad intelligence of the fall of the Alamo, on the morning of the 6th. His letters were dated on the 11th and the 13th, and a letter from Juan Seguín at Gonzales, to [delegates José Francisco] Ruíz and [José Antonio] Navarro, brought the same account. Still some could not believe it.

The sad news indeed was true. Before daybreak on March 6, 1836, Texas soldiers at the Alamo awoke to Santa Anna's army band playing "El Degüello," the song of death. *"No rendirse, muchachos!"* (Don't surrender, boys!) are said to have been the dying words of Colonel William B. Travis, commander of Texas troops at the Alamo. Several hours later, as cannon smoke cleared, at least 182 Texans and Tejanos and perhaps as many as 1,600 Mexicans lay dead. Only a handful of people survived the bloody battle.

Women During the Texas Revolution —

Suzanna Dickenson and her daughter, Angelina, were among those Texans who walked away from the remains of the Battle of the Alamo. Santa Anna allowed them to leave. They were met along the road by General Sam Houston's scout, Deaf Smith, who took them to Gonzales to describe the Alamo massacre to General Houston. But what were the other women of Texas doing during the revolutionary years? They were making important contributions in other ways.

Texans flew this flag over the Alamo during their fight with Santa Anna there. It was made by Texas women to honor soldiers who had traveled from New Orleans to fight in the Alamo.

During those early stages of frontier development, almost all black women worked. Most of them worked as slaves for the Anglo-dominated society. A small percentage of African-Texan women during the 1820s were free, however. A surprising number of them were fully supporting single heads of households. To earn a living, most of them cooked or sewed clothes for Anglo-Texans.

The lifestyles of Tejanas and white women during the revolution were a lot alike. They bore the children, clothed them, and gathered food to feed them. Salt, pepper, coffee, and sugar were about the only supplies the women purchased. They were in charge of households, ranches, gardens, and farms. Their family's income determined whether they had domestic help. Regardless of their economic class, they all learned survival skills for frontier living. They gave their full attention to holding together households and communities. In the words of Martha Mitten Allen, professor of history at Southwestern University in Georgetown:

Women saved the frontier from backsliding. Men were often seen as the heroes for whom the West was a mythic idea, a personal rite of passage. Women, however, sustained the life cycle and maintained continuity and culture. They were the true preservers of the wisdom of the past, which they pieced and stitched into a new social fabric.

Suzanna Dickenson and her daughter, Angelina, survived the Battle of the Alamo, then reported the massacre to General Sam Houston.

Surrender of Santa Anna, by William H. Huddle. Courtesy of the Archives Division, Texas State Library.

Independence and Statehood

As Houston listened to Dickenson's account of the Battle of the Alamo, he realized his army needed more training to conquer the Mexican forces. He quickly retreated with his troops farther east to teach his men military strategies.

On the afternoon of April 21, 1836, while Santa Anna's army napped near the San Jacinto River, Houston's troops launched a surprise attack. The Battle of San Jacinto lasted only eighteen minutes. When the shooting stopped, 630 Mexicans lay dead. Only nine Texans had been killed. Finally, the Texans could claim their independence from Mexico.

The next day Santa Anna was found hiding in the woods. But Houston didn't let his soldiers execute the defeated general. Houston later reflected on his own beliefs and values: "My motive in sparing the life of Santa Anna was to relieve the country [Texas] of all hostile enemies without further bloodshed, and to secure his acknowledgement of our independence."

So began the new Republic of Texas. Sam Houston became the first president. For the next ten years, the new nation functioned as an independent country with its own government. It

During the Battle of San Jacinto, Sam Houston's ankle was shattered by a musket ball. In this painting, he accepts the surrender of Santa Anna. Houston's scout, Deaf Smith, sits nearby, holding his hand to his ear.

even had its own navy. The ideas, beliefs, and values of the Texas culture had triumphed.

On February 28, 1845, both houses of the United States Congress passed a resolution allowing Texas to become the twenty-eighth state of the United States of America. Although Texans had been proud to be an independent nation, they understood the advantages of statehood. United States postal service and military protection seemed especially appealing. They also wanted a secure money system to relieve them of their war debts. On December 29, 1845, the Lone Star Republic became the Lone Star State.

Portrait of Sam Houston, by William G. M. Samuel. Oil on canvas, 60" x 41". Courtesy of the Witte Museum, San Antonio, Texas.

The Lone Star Flag

The flag that flies over Texas today was first adopted in 1839 as the national flag of the Republic of Texas. Its design reflected Texas's name as the Lone Star Republic. Later, in 1845, Texas became the Lone Star State.

Earlier, from 1821 to 1836, however, the flag of Mexico flew over Texas. During battles with Mexico, Texans and Tejanos carried other flags. For example, the New Orleans Greys flag was made by Texas women as a gift to volunteers from Louisiana who fought at the Alamo. Kentucky women made the flag their volunteers carried at the Battle of San Jacinto. It hangs today in the capitol in Austin.

After the Declaration of Independence was signed, both men and women set about to design a new flag. Many people have claimed credit for the design of the Lone Star flag. Joanna Troutman from Georgia is often called "the Betsy Ross of Texas" because she created the first Lone Star flag ever raised. It flew over Velasco, Texas, on January 8, 1836. Troutman's flag, made

Original color sketch by Peter Krag of the flag for the Republic of Texas, approved January 25, 1839

Joanna Troutman

from her silk skirt, had a blue star, rather than a white one, which appears on today's Lone Star flag. After the victory at San Jacinto, the new government of the Republic honored Troutman with Santa Anna's silver spoon and fork.

The Lone Star flag designed by Sarah Dodson from Harrisburg, Texas, looks a lot like the flag Texans fly today. She made it for her husband to carry in battle. In 1836 it flew over the building in which the Texas Declaration of Independence was signed.

Sarah Dodson flag

45

The Capital of Texas

The capital city of Texas — Austin — is its seat of government. It is where ideas, beliefs, and values of the Texas culture become state laws. The capitol building and many other state government offices are located in Austin.

One of the acts passed in 1836 by the first Congress of the nation of Texas was to move its temporary capital from Columbia to the village of Houston. Named for Sam Houston, the small village quickly grew. Eventually it became the largest city in Texas.

By 1839 the Texas Congress and Texas President Mirabeau B. Lamar had become unhappy with Houston as the capital. They believed it was too far from inland cities. Besides, the president wanted to take away this honor from his political rival, Sam Houston.

Lamar's scouts gladly chose the tiny frontier village of Waterloo on the banks of the Colorado River, where only a few families of the early settlers lived. In fact, the first citizens of Waterloo probably were Native Americans.

Today's capital was named for Stephen F. Austin, known as the Father of Texas.

The first capitol in Austin was surrounded by a fence of stout posts as protection against Native American raids.

The Tonkawas had lived and hunted there during the 1700s.

The scouts' report to Lamar described Waterloo as having a heathful climate, fine water, available timber, and abundant stone. It pointed out the central location and the overwhelmingly beautiful landscape. During September of 1839, state records and furniture were transported from Houston to Waterloo in ox-drawn wagons. That same year, the new capital of Waterloo was renamed Austin in honor of Stephen F. Austin.

Today's Texas state capitol building replaced an earlier structure that was destroyed by fire in 1881. Completed in 1888, it's the largest state capitol in the United States. The huge blocks of granite were transported to Austin by rail from Granite Mountain, near Marble Falls. To shape the red granite for the building, sixty-two stonecutters were brought to Texas from Scotland. Beautiful wooden paneling and doors, along with brass hardware and banisters, adorn the interior of the structure.

Today about one half million people live in

Austin. They enjoy exercising in the many parks with "hike-and-bike" trails. They debate how best to preserve the beautiful waters of Barton Springs, a natural swimming pool near the center of the city. A variety of artists — writers, visual artists, dramatists, dancers, musicians — claim Austin as their home. In fact, because of the many types of music played in Austin, the city has become nationally known as a mecca for music.

State, local, and federal governments employ more than one third of Austin's workforce. The capital city is home to the first and largest campus of the University of Texas. Recently Austin has become a manufacturing center for computer and other types of electronic equipment. It has also been selected as the site for several Hollywood movies.

Thousands of people from around the world visit Austin every day. They travel to attend one of the seven colleges or universities within the city, to visit the state capitol, or perhaps to participate in a state band or sports tournament. Some people even travel from afar to observe the nation's largest urban bat colony living beneath the Congress Avenue bridge. For these and other reasons, Texans value and take great pride in their state capital.

Mrs. Eberly Firing off Cannon.

The Archives War

A colorful episode testing the location of the capital occurred in 1842, when Mexican troops once again stirred up trouble by invading San Antonio. By then Sam Houston had been reelected president of the Republic. His soldiers forced the troops back into Mexico. At the same time, Houston ordered the government archives, or records, of Texas to be moved from Austin to Houston. He said he wanted to protect them from the nearby battle zone. Many people suspected that Houston merely wanted instead to move the capital back to the village named for him.

Austinites quickly united against the move. Led by Angelina Eberly, who managed hotels in Austin, local citizens fired on government officials trying to load papers onto wagons. No one was hurt. This brief conflict became known as the Archives War. It ended with the records located back in Austin, where they have remained.

Before the *Goddess of Liberty* was raised to the top of the capitol dome in 1888, construction workers gathered around her. Since then, the fifteen-foot-tall zinc sculpture has periodically been lowered to be cleaned and repaired.

At 313 feet tall, the Texas state capitol stands six feet higher than the United States capitol. Until the early 1900s, the state capitol's elevators were powered by water.

Education for the People

"A cultivated mind is the guardian genius of Democracy." Those were the words of Texas's newly elected president, Mirabeau B. Lamar, in 1838. He believed the new nation should set up a system of public education for its children. The early settlers had listed the failure to provide education as one of their grievances in the Texas Declaration of Independence from Mexico. In 1839 and 1840, the Congress of Texas showed that it, too, valued public education when it passed education acts. These new decisions gave each Texas county 17,712 acres of land for schools.

For the next hundred years, many Texas children attended one-room log schoolhouses. Only one teacher served students of all ages and often enforced strict discipline. Older children helped younger siblings learn to read and write. In some schools, even the young children learned ancient history and languages such as Greek and Latin.

Early Texas schoolhouses had rows of wooden benches and desks that sat on dirt floors. The log plank walls had no windows, so students relied on light shining through the large cracks between the logs. On the darkest winter days they used lanterns and torches instead. As cities grew up at the turn of the twentieth century, larger urban schools came about. Today in Texas, many of yesteryear's one-, two-, and three-room schoolhouses can still be seen sprinkled across rural landscapes. Several of these old wooden or stone structures have been modernized and continue to function as schools. In Doss, Texas, for example, the three-room schoolhouse has served Hill Country students in kindergarten through eighth grades for more than one hundred years.

Unfortunately, not all Texas children benefited from the

In 1917 Jovita Idar established a free kindergarten in San Antonio. She believed in helping children of all ethnic groups. She also organized to fight discrimination against Mexican Texans in South Texas and voiced her support of women's education.

In about 1915, Mrs. Anita McLean taught in this two-room school in Castell, Texas.

education acts of 1839 and 1840. In most cases, African-American Texans weren't allowed to attend the state-supported schools with whites. Mexican Texans were often discriminated against, too. Even without many financial resources, blacks and Mexican Texans formed their own schools. During the late 1880s they began to receive state funding to build so-called "separate but equal" schools for themselves. But the quality of education was, in fact, not equal to that of schools for whites. Finally, in 1954, the United States Supreme Court ruled that public schools could not be segregated by race.

Since 1954 students of all ethnic groups have attended public schools together. All public schools in Texas, grades kindergarten through twelve, follow general curriculum guidelines issued by the Texas Education Agency. Parents and educators working together on local campuses extend the state curriculum to suit the needs of individual cultures.

The Texas public school system is among only a handful in the nation to require courses about the culture, history, and government of its state. In Texas schools, the social studies curriculum in both fourth and seventh grades is devoted to the study of Texas. In this way, ideas, beliefs, and values of the Texas culture are passed along to each generation.

The textbook selection process in Texas is more time-consuming and costly than in most other states. In fact, other states have looked to Texas to make their own textbook selection. The slogan "So goes Texas, so goes the nation" reflects the powerful influence of Texas in the textbook selection process.

Learning to use and understand modern technology and software has become an essential part of the curriculum in Texas schools. By communicating in cyberspace, students can learn more about their own and others' cultures.

Reflecting the culture, Texas education changes constantly. Issues such as bilingual education, arts in education, methods of testing, and prayer in public schools generate heated debates at both the state and local levels. Home schooling and private schools provide alternatives to public schools. Regardless of the way in which Texans receive their education, ideas, beliefs, and values of the culture become a part of their understanding.

The First Colleges in Texas

State-supported colleges and universities didn't begin in Texas until 1871, when Texas A&M was founded at College Station, near Bryan. During the previous twenty years, however, several private colleges got their start. Rutersville College, a Methodist school, was founded near La Grange in 1840. The next year, John W. P. McKenzie founded McKenzie College near Clarksville. In 1842 the University of San Augustine began. Robert E. B. Baylor, a minister, judge, and delegate to the Constitutional Convention of 1845, founded the college named for him at Independence. Baylor University was later moved to Waco, where it joined with another college. Baylor Female College became Mary Hardin–Baylor College at Belton. In the same year, 1849, Austin College at Huntsville was founded. It later was moved to Sherman.

Each year many graduates of Texas high schools attend a Texas college or university. The University of Texas at Austin has an enrollment of about 50,000 students. It is the largest university in Texas. The orange lights on the limestone tower indicate a UT victory in a game or tournament.

Religions of the People

In Texas there are even more religious beliefs than ethnicities. These religions have caused wars, and they have brought about peace.

During the 1500s, Spanish explorers were expected to bring Christianity to Indian Texans. It wasn't until the late 1600s, however, when Spanish priests were sent to Texas to establish missions, that their religion, Catholicism, began to catch on. Even so, many Indian Texans chose not to participate in the mission system of religious reeducation, partly because they had their own religious beliefs.

Early Protestant and Jewish settlers had to pretend publicly that they were Catholic to satisfy the official church of the Republic of Mexico. Only in private could they worship in their own preferred ways.

After Texans overcame Mexican rule in 1836, Protestant churches grew quickly. They became centers of cultural activity. Methodists, Baptists, Presbyterians, and Episcopalians sponsored picnics and fairs to raise money for charity. Protestants, Catholics, Jews, and other religious groups set the moral values of the community.

Today all Texans are free to worship as they please or not to worship at all in both public and private places. This right is guaranteed all citizens of the United States through the Bill of Rights to the Texas and the United States Constitutions.

Most Jewish Texans came from Germany and eastern European countries. They spoke different languages, but they shared a religion from a country that is now Israel. Today Jewish Texans continue the religious traditions passed on by their ancestors. The menorah, a branched candleholder, is used during Hanukkah, a Jewish holiday.

Built in 1682, the Ysleta mission near El Paso was the first permanent settlement built by the Spaniards in the area now known as Texas. At about that same time, the Tiguas arrived in Texas from New Mexico. Today the mission still stands on their twenty-seven-acre reservation.

The Vereins Kirche, or community church, was built by Germans in Fredericksburg in 1847. The octagonal structure was used by many religious groups. Tradition held that women and men sat on opposite sides of the room. The Vereins Kirche stood in the middle of Fredericksburg's Main Street, an architectural tradition in many German towns, until 1897, when it was torn down. A replica of the church (*above*), completed in 1935, stands today in Fredericksburg's Marktplatz (Market Square) as a monument to the original community church.

Servants of the State

For more than a hundred years, many politicians have held office in the capital, where they have enacted laws reflecting ideas, beliefs, and values of Texans. James Stephen Hogg, elected in 1890, was the first native Texan to become governor. His administration is remembered for passing many progressive reforms.

In 1911, Sam Rayburn became speaker of the Texas House of Representatives. One year later he was elected to the United States House of Representatives, where "Mr. Sam" served forty-eight years and eight months as a congressman. As speaker of the House of Representatives of the United States for twenty-one of those years, he was known for his honesty.

In 1927 Jane McCallum was appointed secretary of state by Governor Dan Moody. Her "Petticoat Lobby," as the press called her followers, helped reform government to benefit women and children in Texas.

After holding the state office of treasurer, Ann Richards was elected governor of Texas in 1990. Governor Richards brought new industries to the state, appointed many women and people from ethnic minorities to state positions, and supported the efforts of public school teachers. Following tradition, she left behind a gift in the governor's mansion. The silver necklace from Mexico symbolizes her pride as a woman in having been governor and in the improved relations that she gained with Mexico.

During her term as governor, Ann Richards appointed about 2,400 people to boards, commissions, executive posts, and the judicial bench. Of those people, 43 percent were women, 64 percent were white, 18 percent were Hispanic, and 16 percent were African American.

Richards was followed by George W. Bush, who became governor in 1995. His administration is focusing on welfare reform, juvenile justice reform, ending lawsuit abuse, and increasing local control of Texas schools. Governor Bush's father, George H. W. Bush, who also calls Texas home, was the forty-first president of the United States.

CHAPTER FOUR
~ · ★ · ~ Texans at Work

Making Tamales, from *Family Pictures,* by Carmen Lomas Garza. Reprinted by permission of Children's Book Press, Emeryville, CA.

Work habits and play preferences say a lot about a culture. They form the way people take care of themselves and their families. They show how talents and skills are used to help the community. They reflect the value people place on both tending to business and taking time away from the daily routine to enjoy life.

Early Indian Texans worked as teams to provide for everyone in the group. Men and older boys often hunted meat while women gathered berries, cooked, and took care of the children. Some early Indian Texan groups traded goods as a way of working. As new settlers moved into Texas, they too traded with Indian Texans and other new settlers. Later, the Republic printed paper money as a means of exchange.

Only one hundred years ago, most people still earned a living in the rural areas of the state by working on farms. By 1988, 80 percent of all Texans lived in urban areas. Today crops are harvested largely by machines, and many cattle are fed in feedlots. As a result, fewer workers are needed on farms and ranches. Most job opportunities are in or near cities. The migration of families from rural to urban settings has changed the way people work and live, affecting the Texas culture.

Today Texans work in a variety of ways. The oil industry, government, and service organizations, such as medicine and education, continue to provide employment. Since the 1970s, many workers have made computers and other electronic equipment. Hollywood producers have selected Texas as a setting for films. Theme parks and musical concerts have raised revenue. The passage of the North American Free Trade Agreement (NAFTA) in 1993 has boosted parts of the Texas job market through trade with Mexico. Manufacturing and trade have become fast-growing industries in Texas cities.

Rodeo!

The first cattle brought to Texas were led by Spanish explorers about four hundred years ago. These animals were unbranded and as wild as the deer, antelope, and buffalo that roamed the range. Nobody owned them, and no fences held them in.

Later, in East Texas and along the Rio Grande, vaqueros tended herds of cattle owned by Spanish-speaking rancheros. The cattle provided meat and leather for the Mexican Texans. Spanish cattle thrived in Texas until the arrival of Anglo-American settlers in 1821. Some of the newcomers brought horses and dairy stock with them. The settlers soon acquired Spanish cattle, and some of them crossbred the Spanish stock with theirs. J. Frank Dobie, in his book *Up the Trail from Texas,* explains:

These settlers were usually good horsemen, but they were not used to bucking horses. They knew nothing of the use of the lasso, or of hunting wild cattle in brush. Not one of them had ever seen a roundup — the original rodeo — on the prairie. Just as they acquired cow horses and cows from Spanish rancheros, they acquired the artifacts and techniques of ranching. They took over from Mexican vaqueros the reata and lassoing [roping], a saddle with a horn to tie a rope to, big spurs, leather or rawhide leggings (chaps), and perhaps the broad-brimmed hat. The Texas cowboy who was to trail longhorns up the Chisholm Trail was in equipment and methods a blend of American, Spanish, and Mexican.

CHAMPION BARB WIRE!
(Pat. Nov. 4th, 1879.)

and the **Least Dangerous** Barb Wire known. "A rod for every pound." Send for circular and sample to
179,121,125,127   **HAZARD MANUFACTURING CO.,** No. 87 Liberty Street, New York.

Infringes no patents. Galvanised after being made, it is **Indestructible.** Is the most visible and effective.

The closing of the open range with barbed wire fences during the 1870s in Texas changed the way cowboys worked. It also changed the nature and locations of the rodeo.

As they rounded up the untamed longhorn cattle on the fenceless prairies, those early cowboys often entertained themselves. They rode bucking horses called broncos or broncs, roped calves or steers in record time, and performed fancy tricks while riding. From that tradition, Texans adopted the roundup, or rodeo, as their favorite pastime.

In 1875 barbed wire fences began to be put up across Texas. With the open range fenced off, cowboys no longer needed to round up wandering herds on long trail drives. But nothing could stop Texans from having a good rodeo. Rodeos began to be organized community events.

More than one community claims to have staged the first rodeo in Texas and, in fact, the world. These claims, for example in Pecos and Canadian, refer to the rodeo as it came to be after the closing of the open range.

The first rodeo in the small Panhandle town of Canadian was held during the summer of 1888. It was a two-day celebration. Steer roping contests were the main event. Bronc riding, calf roping, tournament riding, and horse races followed. As is the custom in most rodeos today, work turned to play at a big dance held during the evening hours after the rodeo.

For almost one hundred years, women and girls have added to the fun and excitement of rodeos. Many are contestants in several categories such as barrel racing and trick riding on horses moving at full speed. They have also been known to rope calves and ride bucking broncos and steers. This vintage photograph shows Texas's Tad Lucas performing as America's rodeo queen during the 1920s and 1930s.

During the early 1900s, people gathered at ranch headquarters to watch contestants perform in corrals and later in arenas. Men, women, and children participated. Many cowboys and some cowgirls became professional athletes, earning a living as contestants. They competed on the rodeo circuit throughout the southwestern United States. Today's professional cowboys and cowgirls continue to "rodeo," traveling the circuit and entertaining their fans.

Some of the best bulldoggers and bronc busters are from ethnic minorities. Bill Pickett, born near Taylor in 1863, was of African-American and Indian Texan ancestry. He became well known for the time he grabbed a bull by its horns and threw it onto the ground while another cowboy roped it. At that moment, the thrilling sport of bulldogging was born. After his death from a rodeo accident in 1932, Pickett became the first African American ever to be inducted into the Cowboy Hall of Fame in Oklahoma City. Today the Bill Pickett Rodeo tours the country, showcasing contestants of African-American heritage.

In the historic town of Old Tascosa near Amarillo, Cal Farley's Boys Ranch hosts an annual rodeo. Boys of all ages who live on the ranch compete with one another, along with girls who live at nearby Girlstown, U.S.A. Fans travel from miles around to enjoy this fun-filled rodeo, which recently celebrated its fiftieth birthday.

Women, children, and men from all walks of life and a variety of ethnic and age groups have participated in rodeos. Some of them have been injured for life. Others

During the days of the first rodeos, women owned and managed some Texas ranches. For forty years after her husband's death, Henrietta King owned the best-known ranch in the world, the King Ranch, in the Rio Grande Valley. In the Panhandle, Cornelia Adair ran the 500,000-acre JA Ranch after her husband's death, from 1887 until 1921.

A Cowboy Poet

As a young man, Amarilloan Buck Ramsey worked as a cowboy on a ranch in the Texas Panhandle. One day his horse threw him, injuring his legs for life. Since then he has read many books by famous writers and poets. He has taken English and poetry courses to perfect his writing skills. He now crafts poems that describe his memories of being a cowboy on the range long ago. Sometimes he adds music to his poetry and sings it with his guitar in hand. During the past decade, his fame as a cowboy poet has spread throughout the country. Recently the cowboy poet from Texas was declared a national treasure by the Smithsonian Institution, in Washington, D.C.

Photograph by Wyatt McSpadden

No rodeo would be complete without clowns. Not just handsome, but talented, too — these Boys Ranchers provide entertainment and distract the bulls when contestants are in danger.

In her book, **Chuck Wagon Cookin',** Stella Hughes lists a cowboys' menu served on a ranch in Northeast Texas in about 1868:

Roast venison with brown gravy
Fried catfish (caught from the river that morning)
Squirrel stew
Black-eyed peas
Corn on the cob
Cornbread with fresh churned butter
Cold buttermilk
Wild honey
Plum jam
Sliced cucumbers with sour cream
Watermelon rind pickles

have received only minor bruises. The lucky majority has walked away unharmed. With its wild and woolly nature, the romantic Texas rodeo remains a vital part of the Texas culture.

Boot-Scootin' Boogie

At today's rodeo dances, fiddlers and guitarists play and sing country-and-western music in a nearby barn or community hall. Contestants and spectators of the rodeo magically find their second wind for "boot-scootin'" the night away. Two-stepping, line dancing, polkas, and waltzes keep the action on the dance floor moving, usually in a counterclockwise direction. Before the band bids farewell, everyone jumps in to kick up their heels to "Cotton-Eyed Joe" and the schottische.

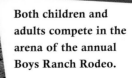

Both children and adults compete in the arena of the annual Boys Ranch Rodeo.

Working on Land and Sea

As this painting by Friedrich Richard Petri, a German settler, illustrates, early settlers in Central Texas knew the true meaning of work on the farm. Everyone — men, women, and children — participated from dawn to dusk.

Most of the food Texans put on their plates comes from Texas farms and ranches. A luscious variety of vegetables, fruits, and grains are grown in Texas. The state is also a big producer of meats and dairy products. Many natural fibers Texans wear, such as cotton, are made from raw materials grown in Texas soil. Leather belts and boots are made from Texas cattle hides, and woolen garments are made from the wool of Texas sheep. Cultivating these and other goods provides work for many people.

During the early 1900s, life on Texas farms wasn't much different from the way it had been during the previous century. Every

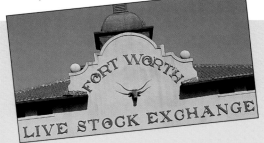

Fort Worth has long been known as "Cowtown." A visit to the Fort Worth stockyards, where cattle are bought and sold, is a reminder of the city's historic ties to cattle trails and the cowboy culture.

By 1873 Margaret Borland owned more than 10,000 cattle on her own ranch. She drove them to market in Kansas, where she died of a fever. Her trail hands took her body back to Texas to be buried.

family member old enough to carry a hoe or milk a cow woke up with the chickens and went to bed with the setting of the sun. During planting and harvesting seasons, parents often kept children out of school to work.

In the early part of the century, few Texas farmers had automobiles, so families stayed close to home for entertainment. Everyone looked forward to evening storytelling sessions, barn dances, and church socials.

Shortly after the arrival of the automobile, machinery began to take the place of most farming jobs in Texas. The size of farms increased, while the number of people who lived and worked on farms decreased. Tractors, combines, plows, and other equipment did the work of hundreds of farm laborers, forcing farm families to move to the cities to find work. At about the same time, new ways of transportation drastically affected the ranching industry. In place of the long cattle drives, trains began to transport cattle. This changed the lifestyles of many Texans.

Today only about 1 percent of Texas workers work directly in agriculture. Even so, with the help of machinery, Texas continues to be a leader among agricultural states.

Some Texans earn their living from the sea, mostly in the Gulf of Mexico. Ninety percent of the catch is shrimp. Also taken are crab, oyster, snapper, drum, and flounder. Each year more than 100 million pounds of fish and shellfish are landed in Texas, at a value of about 200 million dollars.

Fishing is big business along the Gulf coast. This shrimp boat is docked in Corpus Christi Bay.

Grapefruit, oranges, and other citrus fruits from the Rio Grande Valley are shipped northward through Texas and the rest of the United States.

Black Gold!

Without warning, a large volume of heavy mud shot out of the well with the sound of a cannon shot, followed by . . . gas, then oil. . . . The flow increased in force so that within a short time rocks shot upwards for hundreds of feet. Then black oil in a powerful stream, increasing in volume, gushed skyward for more than twice the height of the derrick, crested, and settled back to earth in a greasy shower.

This is how historian C. C. Rister described the first oil gusher at Spindletop, a field near Beaumont, on the morning of January 10, 1901. The derrick and well belonged to Anthony F. Lucas, an Austrian immigrant and a mining engineer. By evening, word of his gusher became world news. The event would mark the beginning of a new era for Texas industry.

"Black gold" gushed at Spindletop, near Beaumont, in 1901. It signaled the beginning of the modern petroleum industry in Texas.

This painting shows Borger in 1926 as it was changing from a "hole in the road" to a prosperous oil center. The rigs went up and the drills went down.

Boom Town, 1927–1928, by Thomas Hart Benton. American, 1889–1975. Oil on canvas. Marion Stratton Gould Fund. Memorial Art Gallery of the University of Rochester. Photo by James Via.

The discovery of oil in Texas affected the culture of the state. It changed the way many Texans would earn a living. It attracted many new adventurers from other lands. Some people became wealthy by drilling wells while others lost money on unwise oil investments.

Since those early years of the oil boom, the oil industry has been the major industry in Texas. Through the years, changes in international oil markets have caused oil prices in Texas to rise and drop. When the economy is strong, most people prosper. But when it's weak, many businesses in Texas fail. From bankers to coffee shop cashiers — everyone suffers.

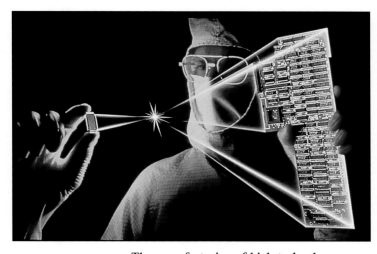

The manufacturing of high-technology equipment in Austin is a recent Texas industry. Many computer companies have relocated there from California and other states.

New Ways of Working

To make up for the problems that come about when oil prices drop, Texas business leaders have set about to attract a variety of industries to the state. They believe it's better not to rely on one major industry to support the state's economy.

An important newcomer to Texas is the high-technology, or high-tech, industry. Satellite communications, computer technology, and cable television companies are rapidly linking Texas with the rest of the world. Several makers of computer and other electronic equipment have moved their businesses from California and other states to Texas. As reasons, they cite an improved quality of life, a clean environment, and lower costs of living. These high-tech industries provide high paying jobs and, in exchange, demand well-educated workers who understand new technologies and ideas. The new industries have helped the Texas economy. They have brought yet another way for people to provide for their families.

The National Aeronautics and Space Administration headquarters is located in Houston. At the Lyndon Johnson Space Center, NASA develops spacecraft and trains astronauts, such as Texas's Dr. Sally K. Ride (*right*), the first woman astronaut.

The Entertainment Industry

Texans love to have a good time. When the work is done, they're ready to play —indoors, outdoors, wherever the action is. In addition to the hundreds of community festivals happening around the state, the entertainment industry thrives.

On hot summer days, people in Texas sometimes pay hard-earned cash to stay cool. That's why many entertainment businesses have grown up around water sources. From deep-sea fishing in the Gulf to white-water rafting in Big Bend to thrilling water rides at theme parks, Texans like to get wet in the heat. Windsurfing on area lakes, swimming at community pools, and canoeing in rivers and streams provide a welcome relief on steamy July afternoons.

Where water resources are scarce, other attractions entertain Texans, along with

On summer evenings, viewers from around the world attend the musical *Texas* at Palo Duro Canyon State Park.

tourists from around the world. At the base of the Palo Duro Canyon, for example, the musical *Texas* has been performed on summer evenings for more than two-and-a-half million visitors. The performance recounts the story of Texas Indians, cowboys, and pioneers of the Old West, telling how they managed to live on the rugged land and interacted with one

---

Let's Go to Luckenbach, Texas

A popular expression, "only in Texas," describes happenings surrounding unusual people, places, and events in the Lone Star State. Originally a German community for most of this century, Luckenbach became a legendary gathering place during the 1970s. At that time, Hondo Crouch, whose business card read "Imagineer," bought the tiny town. Then as now, it consisted of a small general store with a post office, a dance hall, and a run-down cotton gin.

Hondo loved for friends to drop by to play music and dance, tell jokes and stories, and toss washers and horseshoes. Many famous musicians such as Willie Nelson also liked to spend time at Luckenbach. In fact, he and country-western singer Waylon Jennings recorded a well-known song about the town. During the early 1970s, another "imagineer," Guich Koock, served as creative director for a series of Luckenbach World Fairs. Highlights included chicken flying contests, armadillo races, country music, and "down-home" cooking.

Since Hondo Crouch's death in 1976, Luckenbach continues to be a favorite gathering place for music and dancing. It is the site of the popular Ladies State Championship Chili Cook-off.

American Junior Red Cross
volunteers gathered in Weatherford (1917).

Volunteering the Texas Way

Volunteerism has always been an important part of the Texas culture. Without volunteers, many jobs would be left undone. Even though volunteers aren't paid wages for the good deeds they do, they receive a feeling of satisfaction in helping other people and their communities.

Texana Faulk Conn is a Texas volunteer. She has spent about sixty-five years helping the deaf and hearing impaired. At only five years old, she became friends with a hearing-impaired girl named Ella. The friendship would later inspire Conn to volunteer her time helping deaf people gain their full rights in society. Seventy years later, Conn explains:

For many years, the police would send a car out to my house at three o'clock in the morning to take me to the jail, where a deaf person had been imprisoned. I would interpret for the prisoner. My purpose wasn't to get him out of jail. I simply wanted to help him tell his story and understand the charges placed against him. Those are the rights of any other citizen.

Former Texas governor Ann Richards appointed Conn chair of the Texas Commission for the Deaf and Hearing Impaired. Today all deaf and hearing-impaired Texans are allowed an interpreter by law.

another. From the giant stage at the foot of a six-hundred-foot cliff, the music echoes through the canyon as the drama unfolds.

Across the Texas landscape, the motion picture industry is working to provide yet another type of entertainment. During the early 1990s, then-governor Ann Richards supported the Texas Film Commission by encouraging Hollywood producers to shoot films in Texas. Today in Texas, especially in the beautiful Hill Country around Austin, it's not uncommon to stumble onto the filming of a motion picture.

Service Industries

Finally, service industries enhance the Texas culture by improving the minds and bodies of many people while providing jobs for others. Health care workers, teachers, social service workers, and volunteers care for their communities each day. In Texas, about one of every six workers is employed in a service industry.

Health care workers
at the Texas Medical Center in Houston care
for the lives of Texans each day.

Challenges Ahead

Texans enjoy swimming in the natural spring waters of Hamilton Pool in Central Texas. Many Texans and individuals and several organizations are working to protect this pool and other precious natural resources.

Cultural changes present challenges for the future. New industries in Texas, people moving from place to place, and a rapidly growing population require special attention. Threats of pollution, crime, unemployment, and other problems persist in large Texas cities.

With the rising Texas population, basic city services become a challenge. Roads, solid waste disposal, water lines, sewer lines, and police and fire protection must be supplied. Buses help solve traffic problems in Texas cities. Large cities need community centers for recreation. When all of these challenges are met, the culture is improved. People feel safe in their neighborhoods.

Soil, timber, water, air, and other natural resources will survive only if they are safeguarded from pollution and depletion. Many such efforts are underway. Students in Texas schools learn about the importance of protecting natural resources. State agencies, such as the Texas Air Control Board and the Texas Water Commission, are "watchdogs" of the environment. In addition, many nonprofit groups work daily to protect the natural resources in their areas.

Along with urban and environmental concerns, Texans face the daily challenge of combatting crime. Drug abuse and a lack of educational and economic opportunities often lead to crime. Texans fight crime through law enforcement, prison reform, and drug education. Even so, new and better solutions to these cultural problems must be explored.

Large Texas cities such as Dallas present their own challenges. Urban planners and others work each day toward solutions.

Texas Talk

While Texans work and play, they often use speech patterns that seem unusual and even humorous. As in other cultures, language patterns of Texans are learned. They are combined with eye contact, body movement, and gestures. These speech patterns have personality. Some people, such as folklorists, consider sayings that have become a part of the culture an art form.

Talkin' about the weather

Hot enough to cook an egg on the sidewalk = extremely hot

Blue norther = cold front

Cold enough to freeze the horns off a billy goat = extremely cold

Sky's gonna break wide open or Come a thunder-buster. = It's going to rain.

Talkin' about food

Rustle grub = something the cook gets up early to do

Chuck = any type of food

Fluff-duffs = fancy food

Dough-gods = biscuits

Air-tights = canned goods

Talkin' about each other

She don't cotton to that. = She doesn't like that.

Nothin' to write home about = an expression of boredom or disappointment

She's lookin' awful temporary. = She's not staying long.

Plumb gone = departed

Plumb tuckered out = tired

Talkin' about animals

That dog'll hunt. = The idea will work.

Wild as a boar in a peach orchard or crazy as a rusty old lizard or clumsy as a bull in a china closet = to describe someone who's acting strangely

Nervous as a long-tailed cat in a room full of rocking chairs or nervous as a frog in a hot skillet = to describe someone who's uneasy

Ridin' herd = watching over

Yellow dog = someone who'd vote for a yellow dog, as long as it's a Democrat

Talkin' to each other

C'mon and set a spell. = Welcome.

Stop fiddlin' around. = Don't waste my time.

Head 'em up — move 'em out. = Get things going.

Aw, heck = an expression of compassion

How the cow ate the cabbage = a blunt and honest explanation

Talkin' about time

Dark thirty = after dark

Coon's age = a long time

Fixin' to = about to

Shake a hoof = get going

Mosey on over = take your time

CHAPTER FIVE

State of the Art

The Whittler, by David Bates, 1983. Oil on canvas, 96" x 78". Archer M. Huntington Art Gallery, The University of Texas at Austin, Michener Collection Acquisition Fund, 1983. Photo by George Holmes.

Art is a link to the past and a gift to the future. In Texas, as in other places, artists are considered the heartbeat — the spirit, the pulse, the center — of the culture. Through their work, they interpret what has gone before, record what is happening at the moment, and project what may be to come.

The arts in Texas include music, literature, theater, dance, and the visual arts. Texas musicians have mastered just about every instrument and have even invented new ways of playing some of them. Many nationally popular folk tunes — breakdowns, waltzes, polkas, and rags — originated with Texas Old Time Fiddling.

From cowboy poets to epic novelists to writers of children's literature, Texan writers vary in type and talent. Some write purely to make pictures with words. Many have even gained an international reputation. As the late Ada Simond, a Texan writer, explained in 1981:

> *It's a good feeling. It makes you feel humble and introspective and keeps you feeling 'I hope I said it the right way,' because I want to convey the truth. As a writer I want to tell things so that I give a portrait of how things were as a forecast of the way I wish things would be.*

As in other places, Texas audiences enjoy responding to performers. Through applause, laughter, tears — even total silence — they tell actors and dancers what they are thinking and feeling about the performance.

Relics of early Indian Texan artists can still be seen today on walls of caves and canyons. Modern-day visual artists have added their touch to the Texas landscape through sculpture, murals, graphic art, photography, and architecture.

Texans take pride in the many artists who represent their state. Some, such as blues singer Mance Lipscomb or folklorist J. Frank Dobie, are native Texans who chose Texas as their lifelong home. Others, like sculptor Elisabet Ney or muralist John Biggers, moved to Texas from someplace else. Still others, such as painter Robert Rauschenberg or choreographer Alvin Ailey, were born in Texas and moved out of state to create their works.

The Visual Arts

Beginning with the early Native American Texans, every cultural group to settle in Texas has made a visual record of what it has seen, felt, and experienced. In addition to tools such as arrowheads and spears, the early Indian Texans left behind cave paintings and clay objects such as pots and beads. To date, no evidence of a written language has been found. Besides sign language and the spoken word, they used pictographs and petroglyphs to communicate and make records.

Pictographs, or images painted on cave walls and animal hides, served as a type of picture writing. These murals were painted with natural dyes from nearby soils and plants. Petroglyphs are carvings made in stone. Most pictographs and petroglyphs in Texas are found in the western part of the state. From these records, archaeologists have learned about the lives of early Native Americans in Texas.

As colonists flocked to Texas during the early to mid-1800s, many of them made visual records of their experiences. Women stitched beautiful patchwork quilts and wove cloth. Paintings and drawings, such as those by Robert Onderdonk, also document images of colonial Texas life. The Onderdonk children, Eleanor and Julian, grew up to become painters as well. They painted images of old San Antonio. Eleanor Onderdonk served as the first art curator of the Witte Museum there.

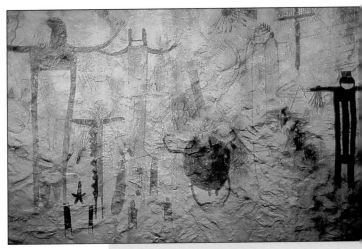

This pictograph was found on a canyon wall in Seminole Canyon State Park. The mysterious figures may be shamans, or healers, in religious ritual dress.

Louise Wueste painted portraits of Texas women during the 1860s and 1870s. Like Eleanor Onderdonk, Wueste faced many obstacles as a woman artist. At that time, art schools across the globe didn't admit women, so those who succeeded often received instruction from a male relative or were self-taught.

Self Portrait, by Louise Wueste. Oil on canvas. Courtesy of the Witte Museum, San Antonio, Texas.

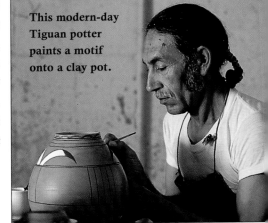

This modern-day Tiguan potter paints a motif onto a clay pot.

Despite the demands put on enslaved Texans, Hiram Wilson and his brother James became successful potters during the last half of the nineteenth century.

Early Texas Architecture

Today throughout the state, many early Texas barns, houses, and other structures from the pioneer days still stand. They remind today's Texans of their architectural legacy from Germany, Mexico, and other countries. Some of the buildings are made of half timber and half stone, a German style of architecture known as "Faltk Vuhrk," or Falk Work. Others are skillfully crafted log cabins made of native trees such as cedar. In the more arid parts of the state, hand-hewn adobe-brick structures made of mud and straw reflect Mexican architectural styles. These and other types of pioneer homesteads are often designated by the Texas Historical Society as official historic sites.

The Old Chisholm Trail, by Clara Williamson. The Roland P. Murdock Collection, Wichita Art Museum, Wichita, Kansas.

Texas artist Clara McDonald Williamson documented cattle drives on the Old Chisholm Trail during the last years of the new frontier. The painting, which hangs today in the Wichita Art Museum, in Kansas, shows the northern end of the Old Chisholm Trail. The scene represents a time when the Civil War had ended, more pioneers rushed to claim Texas land, and the Texas and Pacific Railroad, spanning the state east to west, was completed. It's also a grim reminder of the days when those same pioneers drove Indian Texans from their homelands.

In 1892 fifty-nine-year-old German-born sculptor Elisabet Ney (1833–1907) received a commission to sculpt large figures of Sam Houston and Stephen F. Austin.

Ney selected a cozy Austin neighborhood in which to build her studio of stone and timber. To show her humor and to give a nod to Texas patriotism, the artist designed her stone porch railings to include large copper Texas Lone Stars. From atop the roof, she flew a Texas flag — a gift from children who lived in her neighborhood.

Ney wasn't concerned about other people's opinions of the way she lived her life. Her tiny kitchen was useless for cooking meals. She often ate raw vegetables, rejecting what she called "bloody meat." Inside her studio, from a second floor loft, the artist often climbed through an opening in the roof she called her "sky trap." Sometimes she was accompanied by friends who were authors, musicians, artists, and politicians. They enjoyed visiting with her beneath the stars.

The sculptor's turn-of-the-century home in Austin, shown below, has since become the Elisabet Ney Museum.

Ney's marble sculpture of Stephen F. Austin stands today in the rotunda of the state capitol, with a reproduction in the national Capitol, in Washington, D.C.

As Texas entered the twentieth century, its visual arts flourished. Automobiles rolled in and oil gushed up while architects, photographers, craftspeople, painters, sculptors, and other artists made their mark. Iron smiths, woodworkers, and stonemasons applied their adornments to Texas courthouses, libraries, churches, and school buildings. Texas hatters made hats, tailors sewed custom-made clothes, and boot makers crafted hand-hewn footwear.

In Austin, a popular boot maker named Charlie Dunn (1898–1993) designed footwear from age seven until his death at ninety-five. His customers often had to wait months for their handcrafted boots.

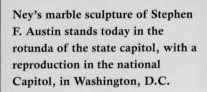

Each pair of Charlie Dunn boots, costing up to $3,000 a pair, had its own appeal. For many of them he designed a motif such as bluebonnets, a yellow rose, eggs in a bird's nest, or a Texas longhorn. Ostrich skins and other exotic leathers ensured a good fit. "That's the secret," he claimed.

In 1981 the craftsman discussed why he continued to make handcrafted boots:

In a factory you do just one or two operations at the most. And that's all you do. You don't go any further from there. You make stitches or soles. You become a part of that machine. And you have just about as much individuality as IT does.

Exuberance! Texas artist Michael Tracy paints from his studio in San Ygnacio, near the Rio Grande. He recently has added video to his ways of making art.

TEXAS VISUAL ARTISTS

John Biggers
Ave Bonar
Jerry Bywaters
Mary Lee Edwards
Jim Franklin
Carmen Lomas Garza
Ana Laura de la Garza
Theodore Gentilz
Glenna Goodacre
Dorothy Hood
Donald Judd
Mary McLeary
Melissa Miller   Jesus Bautista Moroles
Celia Muñoz   Richard Petri
Alan Pogue   Robert Rauschenberg
Porfirio Salinas   Michael Tracy
Judy Walgren

Ilucion Divina I: To Shostakovich, 1991, by Michael Tracy. Gouache, watercolor, and oil stick on water. Reprinted by permission and courtesy of the artist.

As the culture of the state became more diverse, so too did its artists. Some painters, sculptors, and photographers joined national twentieth-century art movements. Perhaps because of Texas's vast size, other artists worked in isolation and developed their own distinct styles.

Many visual artists in Texas have worked on projects together. *Cadillac Ranch* was erected by a group of artists known as the Ant Farm. Located in a wheatfield on IH-40, formerly Route 66, near Amarillo, the landmark sculpture has become internationally known.

Visitors to *Cadillac Ranch* park their cars beside the highway, cross through the gate of the barbed wire fence, and write their slogans and signatures on the Caddy of their choice.

71

THE YELLOW ROSE OF TEXAS

Rhythm and Music

The popular nineteenth-century folk song "The Yellow Rose of Texas" is a part of the Texas music tradition. Likewise, "Texas, Our Texas," the official state song, is known throughout the state. Participating in music—whether by singing a song, playing an instrument, or listening to a symphony orchestra—is a cultural expression common to all ethnic groups in Texas.

Early Native American Texans sang, chanted, and played instruments they had made from natural objects such as bones, horns, skins, sticks, and shells. Music was an important part of their religious celebrations. They marked the harvesting of crops or the successful hunt of wild game with religious songs. Rites of passage such as giving birth, becoming a teenager, or growing old also called for music. Each Native American cultural group had its own musical traditions, many of which are carried on today. As Spanish priests set up missions in Texas, people from Spanish and Native American cultures taught their music to each other.

When colonists arrived, they brought with them a variety of instruments. Each cultural group introduced its own style of music to the frontier. Then as now, German Texans enjoyed *saengerfests,* statewide song festivals, at which people from near and far gather to sing traditional German songs.

During slavery, African Texans used music as a way to communicate among themselves. From their porches, women sang songs with coded messages for other enslaved families to hear. Then as now, church music was also important to the culture. The gospel singing tradition, still popular today, began with African Americans during the nineteenth century.

Young African Texan Scott Joplin (1868–1917) showed a fascination for music. He could pick out tunes on the banjo and fiddle without any formal training. Even though his mother and father were poor, they encouraged Scott's musical talent by scraping together enough money to buy a piano. Young Scott learned to play it by himself.

Joplin later wrote more than five hundred compositions and became known as "The King of Ragtime." Sadly, he never knew of his fame, nor did he realize the fortune that later would surround his ragtime music.

In 1973 Joplin's tune "The Entertainer" became the theme music for the popular film *The Sting.* In 1976, more than fifty years after his death, Joplin received the Pulitzer Prize.

This mural in Texarkana pays tribute to the King of Ragtime.

In 1922 San Antonian Josephine Lucchese (1901–1974) began her singing career as a soprano in New York. The daughter of Sam Lucchese, a well-known Italian-Texan boot maker in San Antonio, she soon became known as "The American Nightingale."

The Buddy Holly Memorial in Lubbock reminds visitors of his innovative rock 'n' roll songs such as "Peggy Sue," "Maybe Baby," "That'll Be the Day," "Every Day," and "Raining in My Heart."

During her brief lifetime, Janis Joplin became well known nationally as a soulful rock and blues singer. This tribute to the popular Texas performer stands in the Museum of the Gulf Coast, in Port Arthur, her hometown.

By the 1920s, Texans were combining many types of music to create new blends. Songwriters and composers transformed traditional folk music into new styles.

During the 1930s, a style of Texas music known as *conjunto* began with Narciso Martínez in South Texas. He combined Mexican waltzes, German polkas, and Czech mazurkas to create his new music. Today Flaco Jiménez carries on this joyful tradition with his accordion.

At about the same time that *conjunto* began, a young fiddle player named Bob Wills of Turkey, Texas, invented western swing. This new type of music was a blend of the many ethnic styles Wills had heard as a Texas youngster. Rural southern fiddle tunes, Mexican folk music, and blues and jazz songs of the African-Texan culture influenced the creation of western swing. Songs by Bob Wills and the Texas Playboys, his band, are known throughout the world.

By the 1950s the music style called rock 'n' roll had arrived in Texas. Many types of Texas music influenced rock 'n' roll. For example, the blues, jazz, boogie-woogie, and folk sounds from African Texans could be heard in the bold new sound.

Van Cliburn

During the 1950s, a Kilgore teen named Van Cliburn (1934 –) won the Tchaikovsky International Competition in Moscow. Instantly he became known as one of the best classical pianists in the world. Today Van Cliburn lives in Fort Worth and performs all over the world. Each year since 1962, he has held the Van Cliburn International Piano Competition for young musicians.

Young musicians enjoy learning Texas Old Time Fiddling tunes. Most of the breakdowns, waltzes, and rag tunes aren't recorded on paper but are passed along by ear. Each year fiddlers of all ages compete in contests across the state.

Texans and longtime friends, Willie Nelson from Abbott and Kris Kristofferson from Brownsville often blend sounds of country, rock, and blues. Progressive blends of music became Austin's trademark during the 1970s. *Austin City Limits*, public television's popular music program begun during that era, continues to showcase musicians from Texas and elsewhere.

Throughout Texas, young musicians launching a career, such as Ian Moore and Eric Johnson, are hitting the pop charts with their own brands of music. Selena Quintanilla Perez, from Corpus Christi, performed Tejano music, which soared in popularity in the early 1990s. In 1995 the internationally known singer tragically lost her life at age twenty-three.

The youngest participants of the Texas music scene are preschool-age children. They delight in the tunes written and sung by several Texas artists such as Naomi Shihab Nye, Carol Perkins, and Joe Scruggs. These writers of children's tunes are known for their lively rhythms and rhymes. Other young Texans enjoy participating in nonprofessional music associations. The Texas Old Time Fiddlers Association, the Texas Bluegrass Association, and local choirs, bands, and orchestras plant seeds for tomorrow's crop of Texas musicians.

The soulful music of mariachi bands is a popular Texan tradition from Mexico.

Sacred Harp Singing

The Southwest Texas Sacred Harp Singing Convention held its first meeting in 1900 in McMahan, where it has met every year since. Without any instruments, singers belt out lyrics to songs in hymnals with notes shaped like squares, triangles, and diamonds.

The sacred harp method of singing began in colonial New England to help people who didn't know how to read standard music scores. Later, during the 1800s, the movement spread throughout the South. Then, as now, any singer — man, woman, or child — can stand in the center of the group to lead a hymn.

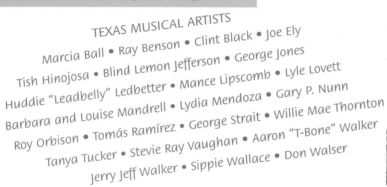

Born April 30, 1933 in Abbott, Texas, Willie Nelson grew up to become a world-renowned singer and songwriter.

TEXAS MUSICAL ARTISTS
Marcia Ball • Ray Benson • Clint Black • Joe Ely
Tish Hinojosa • Blind Lemon Jefferson • George Jones
Huddie "Leadbelly" Ledbetter • Mance Lipscomb • Lyle Lovett
Barbara and Louise Mandrell • Lydia Mendoza • Gary P. Nunn
Roy Orbison • Tomás Ramírez • George Strait • Willie Mae Thornton
Tanya Tucker • Stevie Ray Vaughan • Aaron "T-Bone" Walker
Jerry Jeff Walker • Sippie Wallace • Don Walser

This happy camper enjoys a weekend outing to the annual Kerrville Folk Festival.

The Spoken and Written Word

Anthropologists learn a lot about a culture through the language and stories of the people they are studying. Folklore and tales passed on through the generations are especially valuable types of evidence. Many of these stories were told orally for hundreds of years before they were ever written down.

An important preserver of both the oral and written tradition is the Texas Folklore Society, founded in 1909. Its members have conducted many interviews with Texans from all walks of life. With that information, they have recorded hundreds of tales passed on orally by the early Texans, as well as other folklore from more modern times.

The oral tradition has at some point been the most important way of language communication in almost every culture. As people learned to read and write, some accounts were recorded as books, articles, letters, diaries, and other keepsakes.

Texas folklorist J. Frank Dobie once described the state's Dr. J. Mason Brewer as "the best storyteller of Negro folklore anywhere in America." Because few African-American enslaved people were allowed to read or write, Brewer felt a need to record their oral stories as he learned them some hundred years later. "Old Sister Goose," "Swapping Dreams," "Aunt Dicy Tales," "The Word on the Brazos," and "Dog Ghosts" are among his most popular stories.

Cowgirl and the Letter © Bob Wade 1991. Acrylic and oil on photo linen, 4' x 6'. Reprinted by permission and courtesy of the artist.

J. Mason Brewer recorded the folklore of African Texans. Among his best-known subjects were dog ghosts. According to legend, people who died could come back to Earth as dogs. If a person needed help, she or he could call upon a dog for assistance.

During the mid–twentieth century, Texas's Katherine Anne Porter gained national fame for her writings in fiction. Her novel *Ship of Fools* became an American classic.

More recently, other Texas novelists have received national attention. Who hasn't heard of Larry McMurtry, whose novels *Lonesome Dove, The Last Picture Show, Terms of Endearment,* and *Texasville* have become scripts for movies and television? World-renowned novelist James Michener, while writing the epic historical novel *Texas,* decided he liked the state so much that he made Austin his permanent home.

Texan poets are as varied as are other types of writers in the state. Mildred Crabtree Speer, in her book of poems called *Bootsteps,* describes her first pony from a distinctly female point of view:

FIRST PONY

Mine was
a quilt on legs —
patchwork of heart and brain
sewn with a thread of gentleness —
Old Paint.

Many years before the slogan "Don't Mess With Texas" came about, Roy Bedichek (*left*) was a Texas naturalist known for his writings about preserving the environment. The book he holds in the sculpture is perhaps his own *Adventures with a Texas Naturalist.*

J. Frank Dobie (*center*) is remembered for his humor and his writings of Texas folklore that sought, in his words, "to open the eyes of the people to the richness of their own tradition." He grew up on a ranch in Live Oak County, where he became friends with cowboys of various ethnic origins. From their stories and others, Dobie discovered myths and legends of many Texas cultures. His books made readers aware of the variety in Texas folklore.

Walter Prescott Webb (*right*), a professor of history at the University of Texas at Austin, wrote accounts of Texas history. In the sculpture, Webb is shown standing with his trouser legs rolled up as if he were wading. The sculptor portrayed him this way because he disliked swimming.

Three Texas writers, J. Frank Dobie (1888–1964), Roy Bedichek (1878–1959), and Walter Prescott Webb (1888–1963) have become the subjects of a popular larger-than-life bronze sculpture. *Philosophers' Rock* stands in Austin near the entrance to the natural Barton Springs Pool.

Lubbock native Glenna Goodacre completed the sculpture in 1994. She explained: "Old men in their bathing suits with pot bellies, bony knees, and big toes — the whole concept was a delight." The sculpture captures the joy of friendship the writers share as they enjoy a lively discussion on a rock near the cool, gushing spring that feeds Barton Springs Pool.

Photograph by Alan Pogue

John Henry Faulk (1913–1990), storyteller, folk-lorist, and humorist in the tradition of Mark Twain, was a modern-day cultural hero. He often spoke at community events in Texas and across the nation. He wrote and performed one-man plays. Nationally Faulk was best known as a strong defender of the First Amendment to the United States Constitution. In 1994 the central library in his hometown, Austin, was renamed the John Henry Faulk Library.

This photograph of John Henry Faulk was taken at the Hiroshima-Nagasaki Memorial in Austin on August 8, 1986.

Nationally popular Sandra Cisneros of San Antonio writes about her experiences as a Mexican-American woman. In addition to poetry, she writes novels and short stories. In the essay "Straw into Gold" she describes her impressions of Texas:

I've moved since Europe to the strange and wonderful country of Texas, land of polaroid-blue skies and big bugs. I met a mayor with my last name. I met famous Chicana/o artists and writers and politicos.

Texas is another chapter in my life. It brought with it the Dobie-Paisano Fellowship, a six-month residency on a 265-acre ranch. But most important Texas brought Mexico back to me.

Sitting at my favorite people-watching spot, the snaky Woolworth's counter across the street from the Alamo, I can't think of anything else I'd rather be than a writer. I've traveled and lectured from Cape Cod to San Francisco, to Spain, Yugoslavia, Greece, Mexico, France, Italy, and finally today to Seguin, Texas. Along the way there is straw for the taking. With a little imagination, it can be spun into gold.

Children's book writer and storyteller the late Ada Simond (1903–1989) was a regular guest speaker in public schools. She told many stories about the African-Texan experience. Some of them were about the challenges she faced as a black child growing up in Texas during the early 1900s. Her series of children's books about a young girl named Mae Dee Lewis tells a fictionalized story of Simond's own life.

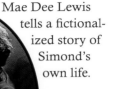

Photograph by Eric N. Hong

The late African-American Texan Alvin Ailey was known for his talents as a modern dancer and choreographer. Even after Ailey's death in 1989, his modern dance company, the Alvin Ailey American Dance Theater, based in New York, continues to tour internationally.

TEXAS DANCERS AND ACTORS

Carol Burnett

Deborah Hay

Tommy Lee Jones

Karen Kuykendall

Mary Martin

Joe Sears

Sissy Spacek

Patrick Swayze

Twyla Tharp

Tommy Tune

Theater and Dance

Any stage — a neighborhood back porch, an outdoor amphitheater, or the grand indoor theaters of Houston, Fort Worth, and Dallas — will do as an excuse for Texans to entertain one another. As entertainment or as ceremony, theater and dance have long been popular art forms in the Lone Star State.

The Kiowas, a Native American cultural group living on the Texas plains during the 1800s, performed a Sun Dance each June. Acknowledging their place in Nature, they honored the sun as the source of warmth and light. Both religious and social dance are still important parts of Native American culture in Texas today.

As other cultures arrived in Texas, they brought their own forms of dance and theater. Rural communities often held dances or dramatic plays in "the hall," the gathering room in a church. As cities grew, Texans erected buildings for the sole purpose of theater and dance performances.

During the rise of the motion picture industry of the 1920s and 1930s, a movie theater was constructed on the main street of almost every Texas town. Stages in front of the movie screens were often used for live performances by actors and dancers.

The fond and familiar lyrics "Waltz across Texas with you in my arms" describe only one among the many dance forms in the state. Today most large Texas cities have their own ballet companies that train local dancers and choreographers in classical ballet.

Folk dancing is another favorite dance form among Texan cultural groups. Mexican Texans perform lively *folklorio* dances in colorful native dress. Other folk dance societies perform dances that originated with European-Texan settlers. In 1991 the Texas legislature designated square dancing as the official state folk dance.

These mimes at the Houston International Festival entertain without words.

At Miller Outdoor Theatre in Houston's Hermann Park, plays and dance concerts are performed for the public.

Keepers of the Culture

The first art museum in Texas might have been something as informal as a hotel room with drawings hanging on a wall. By 1900, however, Houston, Dallas, San Antonio, and Fort Worth had fledgling art galleries for exhibiting and selling artwork.

The one-hundredth birthday of Texas's independence, in 1936, motivated people in El Paso, Houston, and Austin to go beyond galleries and set up art museums. These buildings house art that is donated to or purchased by the museum. Founded in 1929, the massive Panhandle-Plains Historical Museum, in Canyon, is the largest and oldest state-owned museum.

Homes of famous Texans, as well as Spanish missions and old forts, have been transformed into museums. The 1976 United States Bicentennial inspired many historical societies in Texas to set up museums in historic jails, courthouses, railroad depots, and breweries.

Several Texas museums have been funded by single families who value the arts. The Menil Collection in Houston along with the Amon Carter Museum and the Kimbell Art Museum in Fort Worth house permanent art collections.

Some Texas museums, such as the Houston Museum of Fine Arts and the Dallas Museum of Art, house international collections. Regardless of size, however, Texas art museums hold a similar goal — to preserve artwork of the past for future generations.

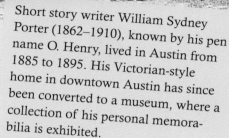

Short story writer William Sydney Porter (1862–1910), known by his pen name O. Henry, lived in Austin from 1885 to 1895. His Victorian-style home in downtown Austin has since been converted to a museum, where a collection of his personal memorabilia is exhibited.

Many of O. Henry's short stories, such as those in his book *Heart of the West,* take place in Texas. During his stay in Austin, O. Henry published a magazine called *The Rolling Stone.* He also worked in a drugstore, sold real estate, served as a draftsman in the old Land Office, and was a teller in the First National Bank.

Special events at the O. Henry Museum include the annual "Pun-off." This afternoon of nonsensical competition keeps the audience laughing at corny puns that O. Henry himself surely would have liked.

The Kimbell Art Museum in Fort Worth was designed by nationally renowned architect Louis Kahn.

CHAPTER SIX

Ceremonies & Celebrations

Dinner on Grounds, by Alma Gunter,1979. Acrylic on canvas, 16" x 20". Billy R. Allen Folk Art Collection. African American Museum, Dallas, Texas. Gift of Mr. and Mrs. Robert Deckerd.

Just as O. Henry suggested, a celebration is always just around the corner in Texas. Parties, fiestas, and other social gatherings provide time for cultural enjoyment. Families and friends break from their normal routines to observe a holiday, perform a religious ceremony, attend a sports function, or take part in a festival.

Early Indian Texans conducted ceremonies to honor seasons for planting and harvesting. Today's festivals in Texas honor seasonal traditions, too. Strawberry celebrations signal springtime. The harvesting of watermelon, peaches, black-eyed peas, cantaloupe, and grapefruit calls for a variety of festivals during summer and early autumn.

Texans even celebrate their homespun recipes. Upon the suggestion of President Lyndon Baines Johnson, chili became the state dish of Texas. Several contests are held each year to prove just exactly whose chili magic tastes best. Chili cook-offs in warm weather and cookie chill-offs when it's cold — any excuse to swap any type of recipe pleases Texas cooks.

Sports in Texas have become another reason to celebrate. Throughout history, children and adults have enjoyed playing and watching informal games. Now all ages participate in organized team sports. Baseball, soccer, basketball, football, track, volleyball, swimming — physical recreation brings Texans together for good health and good times.

Texans traditionally have gathered with friends and family for private ceremonies as well. Family reunions, birthdays, weddings, funerals, baptisms, and festivities to celebrate the beginnings of adulthood are only a few of these rituals in the Texas culture.

I went to Texas and ran wild on her prairies.
—William Sydney Porter (O. Henry), in a letter to a friend, about 1905

SPAMARAMA!

In Austin, people sometimes celebrate the unusual. The SPAMARAMA™ festival has become nationally known. At the all-day event each spring, two thousand SPAM fans create puns, poems, songs, recipes, and even hold athletic contests — all based on the canned luncheon meat with the brand name SPAM®.

The SPAMARAMA™ begins with local entertainers singing dozens of punny songs such as "SPAM by Your Man" (by "SPAMmy Wynette"). Soon the SPAM Olympics begin with the "SPAM Throw," the two-person "SPAM Toss," and speed eating at the "SPAM Cram." Finally, trophies are awarded for the best SPAM® luncheon meat recipes. Award-winning dishes have included blackened SPAMfish, SPAM chowder, SPAM nachos, and SPAM foo yung. Main dishes are topped off with desserts such as SPAMalamadingdong, a SPAM sandwich with whipped cream in the middle, all covered with chocolate.

Throughout the state on May 5, Texans celebrate Mexico's victory over French invaders at the Battle of Puebla in 1862. The Mexican hat dance is a traditional part of the Cinco de Mayo festivities.

Celebrations of Spring

Springtime in Texas marks many beginnings. Even the birth of the Lone Star State occurred during spring. Today's Texans continue to honor the series of events that took place more than 150 years ago. Throughout the state on March 2, many public and private celebrations salute Texas Independence Day, when the Declaration of Independence was signed at Washington-on-the-Brazos. On April 21, in honor of the Texans' final victory at San Jacinto, San Antonians stage a large and colorful festival called Fiesta.

In East Texas, parades, arts and crafts festivals, and fishing and domino tournaments usher in this season of elegant white dogwood and colorful azalea blossoms. *Kindermaskenball*, a German custom, announces the coming of spring in New Braunfels. Police block streets so that costumed children can march through the town playing music and waving balloons. When they reach the town park, everyone picnics.

The annual Poteet Strawberry Festival held each April claims to be the largest agricultural fete in Texas. Area school, church, and civic organizations serve guests strawberry delicacies such as shortcake, cheesecake, parfait, and ice cream. In an interview, Texan Charles Linck recalled a strawberry tale during a time before laws were passed to protect animals. It seems his mother, a strawberry gardener, had been plagued by varmints:

One year . . . the robins would not leave the strawberries alone. Not even a scarecrow kept the pesky things away. One day Charles was alarmed to hear the sound of gunshots. Running to the house, he found his mother standing on the back step,

Track and field events keep Texas athletes, such as UT's Crystal Braddock (*on left*), in good physical condition.

banging away at the robins with a .410. "Mother wasn't a very good shot. We didn't have many strawberries that year. We did see lots of fat robins," he explained.

At the time of the first full moon of spring, Jewish Texans celebrate Passover for seven days. On the first night, at a special dinner called the seder, each family tells the story of how its enslaved ancestors were freed from Egypt many centuries ago. They believe that an angel of death passed over their ancestors' homes, which had been marked with the blood of a lamb.

In Texas, the Christian tradition called Easter is celebrated in many ways. Greek- and Lebanese-Texan children play Easter games with eggs. One child holds an egg while the other tries to break it with another egg. The winner holds the unbroken egg. Likewise, Mexican-Texan children make *cascarones,* colored eggshells filled with confetti. They delight in cracking them over each other's heads.

For about 150 years, children of Fredericksburg have observed Easter fires burning on nearby hills on the Saturday evening before Easter. This Easter Fire Pageant dates back to the time of the early German settlers, when John O. Meusebach had gone to the San Saba River to make a peace treaty with Native American Texan leaders. Indian Texans who had kept watch over the hills of Fredericksburg burned their fires high to signal that peace had been declared.

Several years later, in an effort to calm her children who were frightened of the fires, a pioneer mother added to the story. Her version has become popular legend. She claimed that the Easter rabbit placed eggs in huge kettles of boiling water that sat on the fires. She insisted that the rabbit colored the eggs with dyes of wildflowers. Then she told the children that they must go to sleep in order to find the eggs in nests at the cabin door the next morning.

The Maibaum, or maypole, crafted by artist Roy Bellows, portrays the history of Fredericksburg. It's located in Market Square on Main Street.

Photograph by Jane Cobb

Celebrations of Summer

No matter where you are in the Lone Star State — if it's summertime, it's hot. In fact, on August 12, 1936, in Seymour, the mercury climbed to 120 degrees!

Despite average temperatures in the upper nineties, Texans continue to celebrate special occasions outside during summer months. In addition to observing national holidays, such as the Fourth of July, they get together for

In Corpus Christi, the U.S. Sailboard Regatta each June adds color and form to the beautiful Gulf Coast waters.

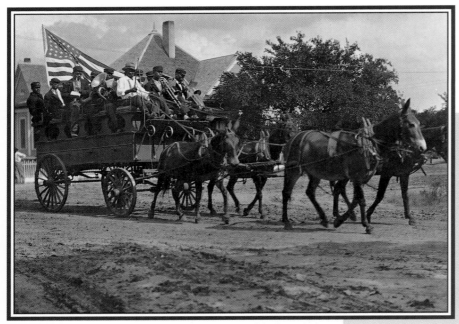

Part of the Parade of the Negro Fair in Bonham, Texas, Hometown of the Photographer, by Erwin E. Smith, 1910–1915. Nitrate negative. The Erwin E. Smith Collection of the Library of Congress on deposit at the Amon Carter Museum, Fort Worth, Texas.

Barbecue—a popular Texas tradition—began in South Carolina, where enslaved Haitians showed planters how to build a framework of sticks for smoking or roasting meat. The planters served it to their friends, who loved it! The word *barbacoa* came to mean both the meat and the social event.

In 1910, forty-five years after General Granger's freedom announcement, these Texans celebrated Juneteenth with a parade in Bonham.

Each June 19 calls for a Texas celebration known as Juneteenth, an official state holiday. On that day in 1865, General Gordon Granger and his federal troops landed in Galveston to enforce the Emancipation Proclamation for the 200,000 enslaved African Texans. Today, throughout the state on the Nineteenth of June, African-American Texans host parades, picnics, rodeos, concerts, and exhibits for all cultural groups to attend. Speeches about freedom ring out from public places. Songs and dances celebrate the rich cultural heritage of the African-Texan tradition.

Then, as now, food was the main Juneteenth attraction. For days ahead, Texans prepared to feed friends and family. The spicy aroma of barbecue filled the air. For dessert selections, people often held cakewalks. Contestants walked carefully with a bucket of water balanced on their heads. Those who didn't spill a drop got a cake.

Recently Juneteenth celebrations have spread to other places. African Americans in California, North Carolina, Georgia, New York, and Washington, D.C., host their own festivities on the Nineteenth of June. They honor Texas's Juneteenth as a symbol of their own freedom.

local and statewide festivities. The harvesting of watermelon calls for the annual Luling Watermelon Thump. Watermelon eating contests, champion melon judging, coronation of the Watermelon Thump Queen, and a Thump Rodeo keep everyone entertained. In 1989 a contestant in the watermelon seed-spitting contest broke the Guinness World Record with a spitting distance of 68 feet, 9⅛ inches!

Nolan Ryan

Summertime in Texas calls baseball players and fans to the nearest playing field. The Texas Rangers are a major league baseball team in Arlington. They were named for the first law officers to patrol the new frontier in Texas.

CELEBRATIONS

Sand Castle Competition in Galveston

XIT Rodeo in Dalhart

Texas Cowboy Reunion in Stamford

Chisholm Trail Roundup in Fort Worth

Shakespeare Festival at Round Top

Stonewall Peach Jamboree

Cantaloupe Festival in Pecos

Texas Citrus Fiesta Parade in Mission

Black-Eyed Pea Jamboree in Athens

In San Antonio, the Institute of Texan Cultures serves as an educational center for interpreting the history and culture of Texas. Inside, the Institute offers hands-on opportunities for visitors to learn about the twenty-seven different ethnic and cultural groups represented on the main exhibit floor. Popular exhibits include the Native American area, with a Sioux tipi; a Mexican *jacal,* with corn grinding demonstrations; and an area with a working spinning wheel and loom. Every year in early August, the Institute hosts the exciting Texas Folklife Festival on its grounds in HemisFair Park. About 75,000 visitors enjoy the contributions of the 10,000 participants, who share their food, music, dancing, stories, and crafts.

Celebrations of Fall

In early Texas cultures, fall wasn't complete without ancient rituals to celebrate bountiful harvests. The most important ceremony of the Caddoes was the Green Corn Ceremony. Festivities were held in early autumn as the crops for the year were collected. For three days, families danced, feasted, and played games. Today the Tiguas in El Paso celebrate the autumn equinox in late September to mark the final gathering of their crops.

Vietnamese-Texan children celebrate Trung Thu, a custom to mark the biggest full moon and the end of the rice harvest in Vietnam. Amarillo and Texarkana hold fairs to showcase vegetable harvests and livestock from tristate and four-state areas.

Some Texans like to ritualize the arrival of autumn by cooking a big pot of chili or stew. Although many stews consist of meat and vegetables from the grocery store, Francis E. Abernethy of Nacogdoches recalls one memorable concoction that he and his hunting buddies put together outdoors when he was a young man:

> *We skinned our squirrels and quartered them and tossed them in the pot. The stock was already boiling and squirrel parts were cooking tender. Somebody had tossed in some young cat squirrels, heads and tails, and they periodically rolled to the surface to see what was coming next. A young coon and a rabbit were added to the pot, and some uncle threatened the stew with armadillo that was snuffling around in the brush just outside the firelight. . . . When the meat started coming off the bones, the cooks — everybody there — added carrots, potatoes, onions, and [who] knows what else, canned or cut.*

Young trick-or-treaters on Halloween might think they're celebrating the harvest of candy, the sculpting of jack-o'-lanterns, and the creation of colorful costumes. In fact, they're honoring All Hallow Even, or Holy Evening, a Catholic tradition held each October 31. Legend holds that witches and evil spirits come out that night, although they must leave by morning.

CELEBRATIONS

Harvest Moon Festival in Granbury

Peanut Festival at Grapeland

Turkeyfest at Cuero

Rice Festival at Winnie

Shrimporee at Aransas Pass

East Texas Yamboree at Gilmer

The holiday Diez y Seis de Septiembre, or September 16, is Mexico's Independence Day from Spain. Texans of all cultures join Mexican Texans in celebrating that day when, in 1810, Father Miguel Hidalgo y Costilla called for Mexico's independence.

86

The next day, November 1, is All Saints' Day. It's followed on November 2 by All Souls' Day, often called El Dia de los Muertos, or the Day of the Dead. On this day, Mexican Texans honor the members of their families who've died. They decorate graves with flowers, pumpkins, balloons, and other festive symbols.

Autumn in Texas wouldn't be complete without the mention of Thanksgiving, a national tradition. Turkey and dressing and family reunions honor the feast of the Wampanoags and the Pilgrims at Plymouth Colony, in Massachusetts. The modern version of this holiday also includes football. Fans look forward to the annual Thanksgiving Day game between the "Fighting Aggies" of Texas A&M and the University of Texas Longhorns. From junior high school teams to the Houston Oilers and the Dallas Cowboys, football fever runs high throughout autumn in Texas.

With a bit of imagination, festival-goers can be officially knighted by kings and lords of the land.

Just north of Houston in the Piney Woods, the annual Texas Renaissance Festival re-creates an outdoor sixteenth-century setting, celebrating a time when the arts flourished in Europe.

Tailgating is a Texas tradition that takes place at the site of a football game before it begins. To avoid the traffic rush, friends and families arrive early and spread a picnic on the tailgate of a station wagon or pickup truck. Buffet style, people stand around and share the meal prepared by one or more cooks.

Texas Stadium, in Irving, is the home of the Dallas Cowboys professional football team.

The highlight of Charro Days, held in Brownsville during February, is the Mexican rodeo.

Celebrations of Winter

"After dinner, rest awhile; after supper, walk a mile." This Texas folk saying is muttered time and time again as the food and merriment of winter months unfold. With Thanksgiving feasts under their belts, people prepare for winter holidays.

Christmas in Texas is a time for cultures to celebrate the birth of Christ in a variety of ways. Many German-Texan families decorate their trees in the traditional style with candles and cookies. Some Polish Texans in San Antonio hold a ceremony called a *Wigilia,* or vigil. At this gathering, everyone is given a piece of the *oplatek,* or wafer, with a Christmas picture pressed into it. Friends and family say, "Peace be with you," to one another. The vigil ends with a Christmas meal.

Nacogdoches claims the oldest Christmas in Texas. Children there reenact the crèche, or Nativity scene, at a local church. The River Walk in San Antonio glows with thousands of luminarias — paper bags with sand and candles inside. In McAllen, more luminarias, caroling, and a live Nativity scene set the stage for the Candlelight Posada. A Mexican custom, *posadas* are verses sung in Spanish. They describe Mary and Joseph's search for shelter in Bethlehem.

December brings the celebration of several other religious holidays as well. During Hanukkah, Jewish families light candles in a menorah for eight days in an ancient celebration of religious freedom. The Blessing of the Animals is a Catholic ceremony in which family pets are brought to the church to be blessed against disaster, disease, and bad behavior. African-American Texans enjoy a national holiday called Kwanza. For seven days they celebrate principles such as self-determination and creativity.

The University of Texas Lady Longhorns often earn a place on the Associated Press's list of the top twenty-five basketball teams in the United States.

On the first day of the New Year, football again reigns in Texas. Some Texans see the classic game of the Southwest Conference from a stadium seat at the Cotton Bowl in Dallas. Most fans enjoy viewing it in their living rooms, however, with a bowl of "Texas caviar" and chips at hand.

Many Asian-Texan families celebrate the Lunar New Year, marked by the new moon in late January or early February. In preparation for the festivities, families clean their houses carefully to symbolize the importance of being free of debt. On New Year's Eve, they enjoy a family dinner. The next morning, children wish their parents prosperity. Parents then give each child an envelope with money inside. The envelopes are red, signifying happiness and good luck. In Houston, a grand parade with dragon floats and costumes takes place.

Texas Caviar

In Texas, as in other places, people eat black-eyed peas on New Year's Day. This custom supposedly brings luck throughout the year. Texas caviar is a popular black-eyed pea relish. Like traditional caviar, in Texas it's considered a delicacy.

2 1-pound cans of black-eyed peas, drained
1/2 cup olive oil
1/4 cup vinegar
1 clove garlic, minced
1/4 cup chopped onion
1/4 cup chopped bell pepper
1 small jar chopped pimientos, drained
1/4 cup black olives, sliced
2 jalapeño peppers, minced
1 tablespoon chopped parsley or cilantro
1/2 teaspoon salt
freshly ground black pepper

Place all ingredients in a covered container. Let stand in refrigerator overnight. Stir occasionally to mix flavors. Keeps well. Serve with chips, crackers, or on lettuce leaves.

Marshall, Texas, lit up for a Christmas parade.

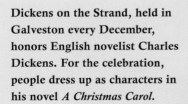

Dickens on the Strand, held in Galveston every December, honors English novelist Charles Dickens. For the celebration, people dress up as characters in his novel *A Christmas Carol*.

89

Celebrations for Every Day

Several celebrations are common to all cultures in Texas and the United States. Every day, birthdays, weddings, and funerals bring families and friends together. Each Texan culture has its own ways of celebrating these occasions.

Everyone loves a birthday party. Children of many Texan cultures borrow from the Mexican-Texan tradition of swinging a stick at a piñata, a large papier-mâché figure covered with bright tissue paper and filled with candies. When the piñata breaks, everyone scrambles for candy. An old-time Texan tradition is to find good luck tokens inside the birthday cake. A dime means you'll earn money this year. If you get a tiny doll, a baby might soon be born into your family. A ring signals that a family wedding is coming up.

Jewish Texan boys and girls on their thirteenth birthdays celebrate their coming of age for religious duty and responsibility. To prepare for the special day, the boy or girl has studied about the Jewish religion. These rituals, bar mitzvah for a boy and bat mitzvah for a girl, take place at a Jewish temple. The boy or girl wears a yarmulke, or Jewish skullcap. A feast for friends and family follows the ceremony.

A Mexican-Texan girl on her fifteenth birthday celebrates her *quinceañera,* a Catholic custom. This is the long-awaited birthday when she passes from girlhood to womanhood. She wears a fancy white dress. Fourteen of her best friends — one to represent each year of her life — also dress formally. They're by her side at the church ceremony and at her party that follows.

Artist Carmen Lomas Garza recalls birthday parties from her childhood in South Texas.

The Birthday Party, from *Family Pictures,* by Carmen Lomas Garza. Reprinted by permission of Children's Book Press, Emeryville, CA.

The State Dish

Chili eaters is some of Your chosen People. We don't know why You so doggone good to us. But Lord, God, don't ever think we ain't grateful for this chili we about to eat. Amen.
— *prayer by African-Texan cowboy and popular cook*
Matthew "Bones" Hooks (1868–1951) at a ranch reunion in Amarillo

The earliest accounts of chili, the state dish of Texas, describe the "bowl of red" as it was sold by women known as Chili Queens. They worked on the square in San Antonio more than a hundred years ago. The recipe began as a way to save money by hashing beef or venison for stew and throwing in some chili peppers and other spices. In those days, chili never had vegetables in it—no tomatoes or onions, and never any beans. Today almost every Texan thinks her or his chili recipe—beans or no beans—is the best.

This notion has led to several annual chili cooking competitions. The first chili cook-off took place in 1967 in the West Texas ghost town of Terlingua. Despite the remote location, 209 chapters of the Chili Appreciation Society sent representatives by automobiles, small planes, school buses, and even jet airplanes. When judges tasted the entries, their faces turned red. Some judges even fell to the floor! No winner was declared. Since then, musical groups and hordes of party-goers meet in Terlingua each November for the World Championship Chili Cook-off.

Pedernales River Chili

This recipe is popular at the White House and at the LBJ Ranch. It was also featured on the Lady Bird Special whistlestop campaign tour during the 1964 presidential campaign.

4 pounds chili meat
 [usually beef or venison]
1 large onion
2 cloves garlic
1 teaspoon ground oregano
1 teaspoon ground cumin seeds
6 teaspoons chili powder
 (more if needed)
2 cans tomatoes with green chilis
2 cups hot water
Salt to taste

Put chili meat, onion, and garlic in a large, heavy boiler or skillet. Sear until light-colored. Add oregano, cumin, chili powder, tomatoes, and hot water. Bring to a boil, lower heat, and simmer about one hour. As fat cooks out, skim it off.

—from *The Texas Cookbook,*
by Mary Faulk Koock

During the late 1800s, Julian Onderdonk painted this scene of Chili Queens selling their "bowls of red" on the Alamo square.

Chili Queens at the Alamo, by Julian Onderdonk, n.d. Oil on canvas. Purchase. Courtesy of the Witte Museum, San Antonio, Texas.

91

Bibliography —

Abernethy, Francis Edward, editor. *Folk Art in Texas.* Dallas: Southern Methodist University Press, 1985.

_____. "Hunters Take Delight." *Dallas Times Herald,* 31 March 1985, A46.

Adams, Carolyn. *Stars Over Texas.* Austin: Eakin Press, 1983.

Albright, Dawn. Texas Festivals: *The Most Complete Guide to Celebrations in the Lone Star State.* El Campo: Palmetto Press, n.d.

Andrews, Jean. *The Texas Bluebonnet.* Austin: University of Texas Press, 1993.

Baldwin, T. B. "How Texas Got Its Lone Star." *Dallas News,* 24 June 1934.

Carlozzi, Annette. *50 Texas Artists.* San Francisco: Chronicle Books, n.d.

Caro, Robert A. *The Years of Lyndon Johnson: The Path to Power.* New York: Knopf, 1983.

Cowart, Jack and Juan Hamilton. *Georgia O'Keeffe: Art and Letters.* Boston: Little, Brown, 1987.

Crawford, Ann Fears and Crystal Sasse Ragsdale. *Women in Texas.* Austin: State House Press, 1992.

Dallas Morning News. *Texas Almanac and State Industrial Guide.* Dallas: The Dallas Morning News, Inc., 1993.

Dingus, Anne. *The Dictionary of Texas Misinformation.* Houston: Lone Star Books, 1987.

Dobie, J. Frank. *Up the Trail from Texas.* New York: Random House, 1955.

Downs, Fane and Nancy Baker Jones, editors. *Women and Texas History: Selected Essays.* Austin: Texas State Historical Association, 1993.

Editors. "Animal Writes," *Texas Monthly* (March 1994): 96–105.

Faulk, John Henry. *The Uncensored John Henry Faulk.* Austin: Texas Monthly Press, 1985.

Flemmons, Jerry. *Texas Siftings.* Fort Worth: Texas Christian University, 1995.

Garza, Carmen Lomas. *Family Pictures.* San Francisco: Children's Book Press, 1990.

Goar, Marjory. *Marble Dust: The Life of Elisabet Ney: An Interpretation.* Austin: Eakin Press, 1984.

Gould, Florence C. and Patricia Pando. *Claiming Their Land: Women Homesteaders in Texas.* El Paso: Texas Western Press, 1991.

Hendricks, Patricia D. and Becky Duval Resse. *A Century of Sculpture in Texas, 1889–1989.* Austin: University of Texas Press, 1989.

Henson, Margaret S. *Anglo American Women in Texas, 1820–1850.* Boston: American Press, 1982.

Hughes, Stella. *Chuck Wagon Cookin'.* Tucson: University of Arizona Press, 1974.

Jackson, Jack. *Comanche Moon: The True Story of Cynthia Ann Parker, Her Son Quanah, and the Wild Comanches of Texas.* San Francisco: R.O.P., Inc./Last Gasp, 1979.

Jones, Nancy Scott. "Chiggers? Try Herbs from 1776." *San Antonio Express News,* 31 May 1976.

Kingston, Mike. *Walter Prescott Webb in Stephens County.* Austin: Eakin Press, 1982.

Koock, Mary Faulk. *The Texas Cookbook.* Boston: Little, Brown, 1965.

Lich, Glen E. and Dona B. Reeves-Marquardt, editors. *Texas Country: The Changing Rural Scene.* College Station: Texas A&M University Press, 1986.

Linck, Ernestine Sewell and Joyce Gibson Roach, editors. *A Folk History of Texas Foods.* Forth Worth: Texas Christian University Press, 1989.

Lowie, Robert H. *Indians of the Plains.* Lincoln: University of Nebraska Press, 1982.

Malone, Ann Patton. *Women on the Texas Frontier: A Cross-Cultural Perspective.* El Paso: Texas Western Press, 1983.

Moore-Lanning, Linda. *Breaking the Myth: The Truth About Texas Women.* Austin: Eakin Press, 1986.

Newcomb, W. W. Jr. *The Indians of Texas from Prehistoric to Modern Times.* Austin: University of Texas Press, 1990.

Patterson, Becky Crouch. *Hondo, My Father.* Austin: Shoal Creek Publishers, 1979.

Pickrell, Annie Doom. *Pioneer Women in Texas.* Austin: State House Press, 1991.

Ragsdale, Crystal Sasse. *Women & Children of the Alamo.* Austin: State House Press, 1994.

Ramsey, Buck. *And As I Rode Out on the Morning.* Lubbock: Texas Tech University Press, 1993.

Robertson, Pauline Durrett and R. L. Robertson. *Cowman's Country: Fifty Frontier Ranches in the Texas Panhandle.* Amarillo: Paramount Publishing Company, 1981.

_____. *Panhandle Pilgrimage: Illustrated Tales Tracing History in the Texas Panhandle.* Amarillo: Paramount Publishing Company, 1978.

_____. *Tascosa: Historic Site in the Texas Panhandle.* Amarillo: Paramount Publishing Company, 1977.

Sinise, Jerry. *Lyndon Baines Johnson Remembered.* Austin: Eakin Press, 1985.

Smithwick, Noah. *The Evolution of a State, or Recollections of Old Texas Days.* Austin: University of Texas Press, 1983.

Speer, Mildred Crabtree. *Bootsteps: Poems of the West — Then and Now.* Amarillo: Paramount Publishing Company, 1978.

Stanush, Barbara Evans. *Texans: A Story of Texan Cultures for Young People.* San Antonio: University of Texas Institute of Texan Cultures, 1988.

Sweet, Alexander. *Alex Sweet's Texas.* Austin: University of Texas Press, 1986.

Texas Department of Transportation, Travel and Information Division. *Texas State Travel Guide.* Austin, 1994.

Texas Women's History Project. *Texas Women: A Celebration of History.* Catalog of an exhibition held at the Institute of Texan Cultures. Austin: Texas Women's History Project, 1981.

Townsend, Charles, R. *The Life and Music of Bob Wills.* Urbana: University of Illinois Press, 1976.

Tolbert, Frank X. *A Bowl of Red.* New York: Doubleday, 1972.

Turner, Martha Anne. *The Yellow Rose of Texas.* El Paso: Texas Western Press, 1971.

Turner, Robyn. *Austin Originals: Chats With Colorful Characters.* Amarillo: Paramount Publishing Company, 1982.

Tyler, Paula Eyrich and Ron Tyler. *Texas Museums.* Austin: University of Texas Press, 1983.

University of Texas Institute of Texan Cultures at San Antonio: The Afro-American Texans, The Belgian Texans, The Czech Texans, The Greek Texans, The Italian Texans, The Jewish Texans, The Mexican Texans, The Spanish Texans.

Urlin, Ethel Lucy Hargreave. *Festivals, Holy Days and Saints' Days: A Study in Origins and Survivals in Church Ceremonies and Secular Customs.* Ann Arbor: Gryphon Books, 1971.

Waugh, Julia Nott. *The Silver Cradle: Las Posadas, Los Pastores and Other Mexican American Traditions.* Austin: University of Texas Press, 1988.

West, John O. "The Galloping Gourmet, or The Chuck Wagon Cook and His Craft." *By Land and By Sea: Studies in the Folklore of Work and Leisure,* edited by Roger D. Abrahams et al. Hatboro, Pennsylvania: Legacy Books, 1985.

Whisenhunt, Donald W., editor. *Texas: A Sesquicentennial Celebration.* Austin: Eakin Press, 1984.

Willoughby, Larry. *Austin: A Historical Portrait.* Norfolk: The Donning Company, 1981.

_____. *Texas Rhythm, Texas Rhyme.* Austin: Texas Monthly Press, 1984.

Winegarten, Ruthe. *Black Texas Women: 150 Years of Trial and Triumph.* Austin: University of Texas Press, 1995.

_____. *I Am Annie Mae.* Austin: Rosegarden Press, 1983.

Acknowledgments

Francis E. Abernethy: "Hunters Take Delight," *Dallas Times Herald,* March 31, 1985. Reprinted with permission of the *Dallas Morning News.*

T. B. Baldwin: "How Texas Got Its Lone Star," *The Dallas News,* June 24, 1934. Reprinted with permission of the *Dallas Morning News.*

Sandra Cisneros: excerpt from "Straw Into Gold" copyright © 1987 by Sandra Cisneros. First published under the title "A Writer's Voyage" in *The Texas Observer,* September 1987. Reprinted with permission of Susan Bergholz Literary Services, New York.

Texana Conn: from an interview with the author, used with permission of Texana Conn.

William Fairfax Gray: William Fairfax Gray diary, Vandale (Earl) Collection, the Center for American History, the University of Texas at Austin.

Bones Hooks: excerpt from a prayer in *Bowl of Red,* by Frank Tolbert. Reprinted with permission of Evelyn Oppenheimer, agent for Kathleen Tolbert, widow of Frank Tolbert.

Stella Hughes: "Chuck Wagon Cookin'" from *Eats: A Folk History of Texas Foods,* by Stella Hughes, p. 95. Reprinted with permission of the University of Arizona Press.

Mary Faulk Koock: "Pedernales River Chili" from *The Texas Cookbook.* Reprinted with permission of Mary Faulk Koock, founder the Green Pastures Restaurant.

Gary P. Nunn: "What I Like About Texas," words and music by Gary P. Nunn. Copyright © 1984 by Nunn Publishing Company. BMI. Reprinted with permission of Gary P. Nunn.

Georgia O'Keeffe: excerpts from letters to Anita Pollitzer in the Yale Collection of American Literature, the Beinecke Rare Book and Manuscript Library, Yale University. Reprinted by permission.

C. C. Rister: from an interview by E. M. Friend in *Oral History of the Texas Oil Industry,* the Center for American History, the University of Texas at Austin.

Mildred Crabtree Speer: "First Pony" from *Bootsteps: Poems of the West: Then and Now,* by Mildred Crabtree Speer. Paramount Publishing Company, 1978. Reprinted with permission of the publisher.

Recipe for "Texas Caviar" reprinted with permission of Texas Caviar, Inc., Austin, Texas.

Illustration Credits

Courtesy of Alvin Ailey American Dance Theater: p. 78 top.

American Red Cross: p. 63 top.

Austin History Center, Austin Public Library: (PICA 07302) p. 16 bottom left; (PICB 07906) p. 47 top.

Sculpture by Roy Bellows, photo by Jane Cobb. Reproduced by permission of Pedernales Creative Arts Alliance, Inc., Fredericksburg, TX 78624: p. 83 bottom.

Courtesy of Governor George W. Bush: p. 51 bottom left.

Cartographics, Texas A&M University, 1995: Map of Texas, p. 5

The Center for American History, The University of Texas at Austin: pp. 9, 16 bottom right, 19 top right, 25, 32 left, 41 screen, 43 bottom right, 46 bottom, and 51 top left.

Hanna Family Papers, Fldr.165, CN95.10, The Daughters of the Republic of Texas Library: p. 53 bottom.

Cal Farley's Boys Ranch: p. 57 all photos except screen.

Fredericksburg Convention & Visitors Bureau: p. 50 middle right.

Gibbs Memorial Library: p. 22 bottom.

Henry B. González: p. 13 bottom.

Sculpture copyright Glenna Goodacre: a gift from Capital Area Statues, Inc., to the City of Austin: p. 76.

Guerrero Photographic Group, copyright © 1993: p. 19 bottom.

The Institute of Texan Cultures, San Antonio, Texas: pp. 13 top right, 16 top right, 18 top and bottom, 21, 36 bottom right, 40 top, 43 top right and bottom left, 48 bottom; courtesy Kathleen Alcala, p. 12; courtesy Mrs. Ron Brown, p. 59 top; courtesy Mr. Florentine Donato, p. 73 top left; courtesy *The Houston Chronicle,* p. 15 bottom; courtesy A. Ike Idar, p. 48 top; courtesy Larry C. Melton, p. 72 bottom right (mural); courtesy Melvin M. Sance Jr., p. 75 bottom; Hal Story, Texas Memorial Museum, San Antonio, Texas, p. 10 right; courtesy Mrs. William E. Warenskjold, p. 15 top; courtesy Mr. Henry F. Wilson, p. 69 top left; courtesy Mrs. Rose Wong, p. 20.

LBJ Library Collection: Johnson family photo, p. 17; Frank Wolfe, p. 31.

The Kansas State Historical Society, Topeka, Kansas: p. 55 top right.

Painting by Lucy Meusebach Marshall, daughter of John D. Meusebach, in Pioneer Memorial Library, Fredericksburg, Texas. Gillespie County Historical Society, Inc.: p. 14 bottom.

Photograph by David Mosher: p. 70 bottom.

National Aeronautics and Space Administration: p. 61 bottom.

National Archives Photo: p. 27 screen.

Courtesy of the National Cowgirl Hall of Fame and Western Heritage Center: p. 55 bottom.

Elisabet Ney Museum: p. 70 top and top right.

Pio Pulido: p. 35 bottom right.

Photo courtesy of Ann Richards: p. 51 right.

San Jacinto Museum of History, Houston, Texas: pp. 39 overlay, 40 bottom right and left.

Susan Allen Sigmon: p. 83 top, 88 bottom.

Spindletop/Gladys City Boomtown Museum, Beaumont, Texas: p. 60 left.

Star of the Republic Museum, photo by H. K. Barnett: p. 45 bottom right.

The Texas Collection, Baylor University, Waco, Texas: p. 22 top.

Texas Department of Commerce/Tourism: pp. 11 bottom; 13 top left; 23 screen; 26 top; 29 top left, top right, and bottom left; 28; 30 bottom three photos; 32 top right, middle right, and bottom right; 33 bottom right; 34 bottom; 35 top left, top middle, and bottom left; 36 middle; 37 top right; 41 overlay; 42 screen; 47 bottom right; 49; 50 bottom left; 51 screen; 53 top; 54 all; 55 top left, middle right; 58 bottom left and right; 59 bottom left and right; 61 top; 62 top and bottom; 63 bottom; 64 top and bottom; 68 top right and bottom right; 70 middle; 72 bottom right (Joplin photo); 73 top right, middle right, and bottom; 74 top and middle; 78 bottom left and right; 79 all; 82 bottom; 84 top right; 85 middle left, bottom left, and right; 86; 87 bottom; 88 top; 89 both photos; 91 top left; photo by Richard Reynolds, p. 36 top left.

Texas Department of Transportation: pp. 23 top, 29 middle right, 45 middle left, 59 middle left, and 82 top.

The Texas Memorial Museum: courtesy of Russell Fish III, p. 58 top; photograph by Billy Moore, p. 33 top.

Courtesy of the Texas Rangers: p. 85 top.

Archives Division, Texas State Library: pp. 39 underlay, 45 bottom left, 46 top right, 47 bottom left, 67, 72 top underlay and overlay.

Robyn Montana Turner: pp. 26 bottom, 27 bottom, 37 screen, 50 top, 57 screen, 69 screen, 71 bottom, 74 bottom right, 77 right, and 87 top two photos.

Western History Collections, University of Oklahoma Library: p. 11 top.

Yale Collection of Western Americana, Beinecke Rare Book and Manuscript Library: p. 19 top left.

Index —